647 Really Weird Facts

THAT WILL BOGGLE YOUR BRAIN

ARCTURUS

This edition published in 2024 by Arcturus Publishing Limited
26/27 Bickels Yard, 151–153 Bermondsey Street,
London SE1 3HA

Illustrator: Luke Séguin-Magee
Authors: Anne Rooney, William Potter, Ben Hubbard, Adam Phillips,
   Clare Hibbert, and Helen Otway
Designer and Editor: Lucy Doncaster
Design Manager: Jessica Holliland
Managing Editor: Joe Harris

ISBN: 978-1-3988-4204-5
CH012100NT
Supplier 29, Date 0424, PI 00006070

Printed in China

CONTENTS

INTRODUCTION

Calling all curious kids! Prepare to embark on a journey through the weird and wonderful world of strange-but-true facts that are sure to make your brain boggle.

First, we'll take a deep dive into the mysteries of the human body in all its gory glory. Discover why snot is sticky and sweat smells, how we fart and what belly buttons are really for. We'll also scratch beneath the surface and take a closer look at the secret lives of the millions of tiny mites, bacteria, and bugs that live on and inside our bodies, and how they can both help and harm us.

Next, it's time to turn to the even more amazing animal kingdom, from the residents of the deepest oceans to the inhabitants of the highest peaks. Make like a shark, and glide through the pages gobbling up tantalizing tidbits as you read all about walking fish, burrowing owls, and sleepy snails.

But hold on tight, because our journey isn't over yet! Step back in time to a prehistoric era when herds of giants roamed the planet and terrifying titans lurked beneath the waves. Unearth jaw-dropping facts about these compelling creatures, from the smallest bird-sized beasts to the fanged, feathered, and frilled brutes that ruled supreme in a land of fire.

Finally, it's back to the future as we surge into the wacky world of scientific discoveries. Explore more about our modern lives, from how deodorants work to what robot kangaroos and tadpoles are used for. We also head into space, past black holes and blue moons, to sneak a peek at how astronauts poop and figure out which planet is best for birthdays.

So, what are you waiting for? Buckle up and get set for the ride of your life.
It's going to be out of this world!

BIZARRE BODIES

DID YOU KNOW?

You have more bacteria on your body than there are people in the world.

HOW FAST IS A SNEEZE?

When you sneeze, the air coming out of your nose and mouth travels at the same speed as a Category 2 hurricane: 160 km/h (100 mph)!

HOW DO ASTRONAUTS BRUSH THEIR TEETH?

In space, astronauts use specially formulated nontoxic toothpaste, because they have to swallow all the froth. Gross!

WHAT'S BETTER, SMELL OR TASTE?

Your sense of smell is 10,000 times more sensitive than your sense of taste. About 80 percent of what you taste comes from what you can smell, which is why you don't taste much at all if you have a cold!

WHAT'S THE POINT OF YAWNING?

Yawning is your body's way of getting more oxygen into your lungs to try and make you feel more awake.

DID YOU KNOW?

Your fingerprints, palm prints, tongue print, toe prints, and sole prints are all unique!

ARE POISONS GOOD FOR THE SKIN?

Poisons can give you great-looking skin! Botulinum toxin (Botox) is famous for its wrinkle-smoothing effects, but for those who don't like needles, there is a cream that mimics viper venom and gives similar results.

WHY ARE FARTS NOISY?

What you hear when you fart is the vibration of your sphincter muscles as air passes through them. The sort of sound you get depends on how fast the air is going.

DID YOU KNOW?

Humans live longer than any other mammals on the planet.

DO YOU SWEAT ALL THE TIME?

You sweat all day long, even when you don't feel it. As you read this, more than 2 million sweat glands around your body are working to keep it at the right temperature.

HOW MUCH SKIN DO YOU GROW?

Your body makes a new skin every month—that means you'll get through about 1,000 skins in your lifetime!

DO SOME PEOPLE HAVE TONGUES LIKE SNAKES?

The most bizarre cosmetic procedure has to be tongue-splitting. A cut is made down the middle of the tongue to give it a forked appearance. Freaky!

IS BIRD POOP GOOD FOR YOU?

Fancy a Japanese bird poop facial? The special enzymes in the droppings of the Japanese bush warbler make it an ingredient in some anti-wrinkle treatments.

WHY IS SNOT STICKY?

Another word for snot is mucus. Mucus is made by cells in many parts of your body, including your nose, lungs, and digestive system. It's sticky because its job is to trap things that shouldn't be in your body—such as harmful bacteria, pollen, dust, and fungi.

WHY DO THINGS LOOK BLURRY UNDERWATER?

The lenses in your eyes are designed to focus the light in air. Water bends light so that your eyes can't focus it properly— that's why everything's blurred if you keep your eyes open underwater!

WHY DO YOUR LIPS GET DRY?

Sebum is the oily stuff secreted by glands in your skin to keep it soft. The only part of your body that doesn't have any is your lips—that's why they dry out easily.

HOW MUCH TIME DO WE SPEND KISSING?

Over your lifetime, you will spend a whole two weeks kissing—though hopefully not all at once!

CAN YOU GROW SKIN IN A LAB?

A new sheet of skin can be grown from just a few of your cells. New skin is grown in special laboratories and is used to replace damaged skin in a skin graft operation.

WHY IS SWEAT SMELLY?

Sweat is made mainly of water, so it doesn't smell ... until it's been around for a while. Once skin bacteria have had time to slurp it up and multiply, the whiff begins.

DID YOU KNOW?

If you cut yourself, your body will produce more than a million extra cells each hour until the wound heals.

WHAT IS A BELLY BUTTON?

Your belly button is the scar left from your umbilical cord. Whether it's an "innie" or an "outie" depends on the shape and size of your umbilical cord when you were born.

WHO HAS THE MOST HAIR— BLONDES OR BRUNETTES?

Fair-haired people have more hairs on their head than dark-haired people.

ARE ALL TEARS THE SAME?

Your eyes produce three kinds of tears—basal tears to keep the eyes moist, reflex tears when you get something in your eyes, and psychic tears when you cry with sadness, happiness, or pain.

CAN YOU GROW TEETH IN A LAB?

Yes, scientists have found a way to grow teeth! So far, only parts of a tooth have been grown from stem cells, but farmed teeth could replace false ones in the future.

HOW LONG DO TASTE BUDS LAST?

Each of your taste buds lasts for just over a week! They are most quickly replaced when you are young.

DID YOU KNOW?

Your nails grow more quickly as you get older.

IS IT NORMAL TO HAVE SWEATY FEET?

Yes. In fact, the 250,000 sweat glands in your feet make them one of the sweatiest parts of your body. Adults produce two whole cups of that stinky foot juice every week!

IS ALL FAT THE SAME?

You have two types of fat under your skin and around your organs—white adipose tissue and brown adipose tissue. They both keep you warm, but the brown fat gives extra insulation, so you had more of it when you were born than you do now.

WHY DO DENTISTS HAVE TO SCRAPE YOUR TEETH?

It takes six hours for a coating of plaque to form after brushing your teeth. If you don't brush it off, it eventually becomes tartar—a rock-hard substance that your dentist has to scrape off.

DID YOU KNOW?

You have a whole nervous system just to control your bowels.

HOW MUCH DO YOU FLAKE?

In the last minute, at least 40,000 dead skin cells came off your body. You lose about 50 million of them every day. If your dead skin cells didn't drop off, after three years your skin would be as thick as an elephant's!

DID YOU KNOW?

Right-handed people tend to chew food on the right side of their mouth, and left-handed people chew more on the left.

HOW MANY PEOPLE HAVE EXTRA FINGERS AND TOES?

Around 0.2 percent of the world's population have an extra finger or toe. That's 12 million people with an extra digit or two!

HOW MUCH HAIR DO YOU LOSE EACH DAY?

Each hair on your head grows for up to six years. Then it stops, hangs around for a while, and eventually drops out. About 50–100 hairs drop out of your head every day, but that still leaves you with more than 99,900 to brush while new ones grow!

DO ONLY TONGUES HAVE TASTE BUDS?

Taste buds aren't just on your tongue—there are more than 2,000 of your them in your throat and on the roof of your mouth.

CAN YOU FREEZE YOUR BODY AFTER DEATH?

People can choose to have their bodies deep-frozen after death in case scientists come up with a way of bringing them back to life ... but they will have to pay around £150,000/$200,000 for the privilege.

WHY DOES BLUSHING MAKE YOU FEEL HOT?

You feel hot when you blush because you're blushing all over! Embarrassment triggers a rush of blood through all your blood vessels, even the ones in your stomach.

DO ANY ANIMALS HAVE FINGERPRINTS LIKE OURS?

A koala's fingerprints look very similar to a human's. If a crime scene smells of eucalyptus, it was definitely the koala that did it!

WHERE IN YOUR BODY IS THERE NO BLOOD?

Your eye's cornea is the only part of your body that has no blood supply, since it needs to be clear for you to see through it. What it does have is lots of nerve endings—that's why a scratch in your eye is so painful.

DID YOU KNOW?

A dead body has to be put in a refrigerator, so it doesn't go off! Bodies in a morgue are kept at a temperature of 2-4°C (35-39°F).

IS HAIR ALIVE?

The hairs that you can see are dead, which is why it doesn't hurt when you have a haircut. They have sensors on the roots, though, so it hurts if someone pulls them!

DO EARS KEEP ON GROWING?

Although your ears will grow throughout your life, your hearing will just get worse. What a bad design!

CAN YOUR HAIR TURN WHITE FROM SHOCK?

It's impossible for hair to turn white from shock. What can happen, though, is that a shock makes pigmented hair suddenly fall out, so someone with a mixture of brown and white hair would then be left with only white hairs.

DID YOU KNOW?
Your teeth are protected by enamel, which is the hardest substance in your body.

HOW FAST DO BEARDS GROW?

Men need to shave so often because beard hair grows faster than any other body hair. If a man let his beard grow forever, it could reach a length of more than 9 m (28 ft).

WHO BLINKS THE MOST?

Over your lifetime, you will blink 650 million times. Women blink more than men, and adults blink more than children. Newborn babies blink only once or twice a minute!

ARE GORILLAS HAIRIER THAN HUMANS?

Humans and gorillas are both covered with around 5 million hairs; the difference is that ape hair is much thicker and longer.

HOW LONG HAVE HUMANS HAD TATTOOS?

Tattoos have been around for thousands of years—there were 57 on the body of a mummified man discovered in the Austrian Alps dating from 3300 BCE.

DID YOU KNOW?

Being too hot or too cold in bed increases your chances of having bad dreams.

CAN YOU DRINK YOUR OWN PEE?

There are no harmful bacteria in fresh urine, so it's perfectly safe to drink. Safe? Yes. Disgusting? Absolutely!

DO WE HAVE METAL BODIES?

You have several different metals in your body, such as iron in your blood and potassium in your nervous system. Calcium is what you have the most of—that's what makes your bones and teeth hard.

DID YOU KNOW?

Your body is made up of more than 230 joints.

DO ATHLETES HAVE BIGGER HEARTS?

People who exercise too much can develop "athletic heart syndrome," where the heart becomes enlarged from having to pump extra blood around the body.

ARE SOME OF YOUR MUSCLES OUT OF CONTROL?

You can control some of your muscles, but others are doing their own thing! Your involuntary muscles control bodily functions, such as heartbeat and digestion.

HOW CAN YOU TRAIN TO BE A SWORD-SWALLOWER?

Sword-swallowers train themselves to control the gag reflex that occurs when something touches the soft palate at the back of the mouth. If you touch it, you'll vomit ... so don't try it!

DO WE HAVE TAILS?

You have a tailbone at the end of your spine! It is called the coccyx—meaning "cuckoo"—because it looks like a cuckoo's beak.

DID YOU KNOW?

If a person's liver stops working, they will die within 24 hours.

HOW MUCH DUST DO YOU SWALLOW?

You will breathe in around 18 kg (40 lb) of dust over your lifetime—that's about 18 large bags of flour!

DO YOU LOSE BONES AS YOU GROW UP?

Yes! When you were born, you had more than 300 bones, but you'll have only 206 by the time you finish growing! Don't worry, you won't completely lose them along the way—some of your smaller bones just fuse together to make bigger bones.

HOW LONG ARE YOUR INTESTINES?

If you took out your intestines and uncoiled them, they would be about four times as tall as you.

DID YOU KNOW?

When you feel thirsty, your body is already dehydrated. It's your brain's way of telling you to get a drink, quick!

DO DEAD BODIES FART?

When a dead body is decomposing, the bacteria inside it produce gases. When the gas is released from the body, it sounds like a fart!

DO BRAINS FLOAT?

Your brain is surrounded by a liquid called cerebrospinal fluid. It cushions the brain to protect it from bumps and sudden movements. It constantly needs topping up, so fluid is being made by your body all the time.

DID YOU KNOW?

Make your hand into a fist—that's how big your heart is!

WHY IS PUKE GREEN?

When you have a bad tummy bug, you will eventually throw up green vomit. The shade comes from bile, which is deep down in the stomach and comes up only when nothing else is left.

CAN YOUR BRAIN FEEL PAIN?

The brain cannot feel pain, so some brain surgery can be done while the patient is awake! The surgeon will then talk to the patient during the operation to make sure that healthy parts of the brain are not being affected.

DID YOU KNOW?

You have three types of ribs—true ribs are attached to your spine and breastbone, false ribs are attached to your spine and lowest true ribs, and floating ribs are attached to only the spine. No spare ribs, though!

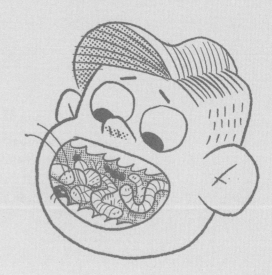

ARE THERE BUGS IN YOUR BODY?

Yes—if you mean bacteria! There are actually more than 700 kinds of bacteria lurking in your intestine.

WHAT DO BRAINS FEEL LIKE?

If you could open up your skull and touch your brain, it would feel like jelly!

CAN YOU HAVE EXTRA KIDNEYS?

You probably have two kidneys ... but you could have more. People with extra kidneys don't find out until they have a scan for other problems. British teenager Laura Moon discovered she had four kidneys when she had a scan for stomach pains!

WHAT HAPPENS IF YOU RUN UP A MOUNTAIN?

Your body is used to the oxygen levels around you and needs time to get used to any changes. If you go up a mountain too quickly, your body will react to the sudden drop in oxygen by throwing up.

CAN HUMANS USE PIG HEARTS?

Pig hearts are similar to ours, so pig heart valves are sometimes used in open-heart surgery to replace faulty human ones.

DID YOU KNOW?

Your body cannot digest tomato seeds—they pass straight through your intestines. Eat some today and see for yourself!

WHAT IS THE LONGEST BONE IN YOUR BODY?

The longest bone in your body is your femur, or thighbone. The thighbone of the tallest man ever was around 72 cm (2 ft 5 in) long!

WHY DOES ASPARAGUS MAKE YOUR PEE SMELL?

If you eat asparagus, your urine might smell of rotten cabbages! The whiff comes from a gas called methanethiol, which is produced when you digest the vegetable.

HOW OFTEN DO YOU SWALLOW?

You swallow between 500 and 700 times a day.

IS THERE A POOP CHART?

If you ever want to classify what you leave behind in the toilet, you should take a look at the Bristol Stool Chart. The seven types of stool listed range from "separate hard lumps, like nuts" (Type 1) to "entirely liquid" (Type 7).

DID YOU KNOW?

There is so much electrical activity going on in your brain that you could power a light bulb with it!

DO SURGEONS LEAVE THINGS INSIDE BODIES?

Foreign bodies can occasionally get left behind during operations. Things that have been sewn inside patients include clamps, surgical sponges, scalpels, scissors, and forceps.

WHAT DOES THE INSIDE OF AN INTESTINE LOOK LIKE?

The inside of your small intestine looks like it is covered with tiny fingers! These villi give your intestine the largest possible surface area for you to get the maximum amount of nutrition from your food.

ARE HUMAN BRAINS BIGGER THAN THEIR ANCESTORS'?

Our brains are three times bigger than those of our ancestors who lived 2.5 million years ago.

HOW LONG DOES FOOD STAY IN YOUR BODY?

Most of the food you eat spends between one and three hours in your stomach, but fatty foods hang around for longer.

HOW ACIDIC IS YOUR STOMACH?

The pH level in your stomach is 1 or 2, which is more acidic than vinegar. Although your gastric juices contain powerful acids, they cannot digest chewing gum. Small amounts will get through the digestive system, but too much can cause a serious blockage ... so always spit it out.

WHAT IS HEARTBURN?

Heartburn has nothing to do with the heart. It's the burning pain of stomach acid leaking back into your gullet, or food pipe.

DO YOU JUMP IN YOUR SLEEP?

If you ever jump suddenly when you're falling asleep, you're experiencing a hypnic jerk. As your body relaxes, the brain mistakes the nerve messages for a falling sensation, and it stiffens the body to get it upright again.

HOW MANY MUSCLES DO YOU HAVE?

You have more than 630 muscles in your body. Even if you're sitting still, lots of muscles are working to do things like make you breathe and keep your blood flowing. Reading this uses your eye muscles, too!

DID YOU KNOW?

A pinhead-sized piece of your brain contains 60,000 nerve cells called neurons.

HOW FAST IS A COUGH?

When you cough, air rushes through your windpipe at 100 km/h (60 mph).

HOW FAST ARE NERVE SIGNALS?

Nerve signals travel incredibly fast—a nerve message from your toe will reach your brain in less than one-hundredth of a second.

WHAT'S A "BRAIN FREEZE?"

A "brain freeze" headache occurs when cold food or drink in your mouth triggers a nerve message to the brain that says you're in a cold environment. Your blood vessels suddenly swell to warm you up ... and it hurts!

DID YOU KNOW?

After being removed from the body, the lungs can survive longer than any other organ.

HOW CAN LAUGHING HELP YOU BEAT A TEST?

Laughing cancels out the hormones in your body that make you feel stressed, so if you have a test coming up, just laugh about it!

HOW DO YOU VOMIT?

When you vomit, the muscles in your stomach and intestines go into reverse—instead of pushing the food down, they push it up and out of your mouth.

WHAT DO HEAD LICE FEED ON?

Head lice slurp blood from your scalp! Don't panic, they're so tiny that you won't feel a thing. Girls are more likely to have head lice than boys, since they tend to have longer hair.

DID YOU KNOW?

A spitting cobra will defend itself by shooting poison into an attacker's eyes, causing agonizing pain and leaving them temporarily blind.

ARE THERE EGGS IN YOUR CLOTHES?

African tumbu flies lay their eggs in clothing. The eggs hatch on contact with human skin, and the larvae burrow under the skin's surface, creating boil-like sores to grow in.

ARE THERE BLOODSUCKERS IN YOUR BED?

Bedbugs are the vampires of the pest world— they hate sunlight and prefer to venture out to bite you at night.

DO BATS LIKE UNDERWEAR?

When hotel receptionist Abbie Hawkins felt something moving on her chest while she was at work, she had a look and found a baby bat nestled inside her bra! The bat-hiding underwear had been left on the washing line the previous night.

WHAT SMELL DO MOSQUITOES HATE?

Mosquitoes hate the smell of garlic, so you can try eating some to keep them at bay. Plus, you can ward off vampires at the same time!

DID YOU KNOW?

Some tapeworm eggs can grow into a cyst as large as a grapefruit! It's not common, though, so don't have nightmares.

HOW LONG CAN TAPEWORMS GROW?

A broad tapeworm can grow in the intestine for decades, reaching a length of 10 m (33 ft). Worst of all, you may not even know you have one!

DOES EVERYONE CARRY PARASITES?

Parasites are happily living in at least 75 percent of the world's population.

CAN YOU GET BUGS IN YOUR EYEBROWS?

Demodex mites are tiny parasites that live in eyebrows and eyelashes. They're very common, especially in older people. Under a microscope, they look like worms with stubby legs.

WHY SHOULD YOU BEWARE OF RAT PEE?

Weil's disease is a serious infection carried in rats' urine. It is usually caught from infected water.

CAN HUMAN POOP BE USED FOR FERTILIZER?

Human sewage is sometimes used to fertilize fields in developing countries, but it can be full of worm eggs. When the egg-infested vegetables are eaten, worm infections are spread even further.

COULD A FURRY CATERPILLAR MAKE SOMEONE BLEED TO DEATH?

Yes. The venom released by the hairs on a South American silk moth caterpillar keeps blood from clotting. As a result, an unlucky human victim could bleed to death if bitten.

DID YOU KNOW?

Bedbugs and fleas can live in your house for a whole year without feeding.

WHAT CAUSES A ZIGZAG PATTERN ON YOUR SKIN?

The tiny scabies mite tunnels beneath the skin in a zigzag shape, causing unbearable itching.

HOW MANY KINDS OF MOSQUITOES ARE THERE?

Too many! There are more than 2,500 types of mosquitoes worldwide. They tend to live in hot, humid places.

ARE THERE BUGS THAT EAT SKIN?

Harvest mite larvae are tiny orange parasites that love to eat your skin. They inject digestive juices into you to make a well of liquefied skin cells that they can then suck up, then drop off when they're done.

DID YOU KNOW?

Helminthophobia is a fear of getting worms. Hands up anyone who isn't scared!

ARE ELEPHANTS TO BLAME FOR ELEPHANTIASIS?

No. The Wuchereria parasitic worm causes elephantiasis, a disfiguring disease where the limbs swell alarmingly and the skin thickens and becomes ulcerated.

HOW LONG DO LICE LIVE FOR?

Each female head louse lives for about a month and can lay up to 150 eggs in that time.

WHAT IS THE WORST KIND OF WORM TO GET?

The worst worm infection you can get has to be tropical Guinea worm disease. Between one and two years after drinking infected water, a spaghetti-like worm up to 100 cm (40 in) long will pop out of a blister in the foot or leg. The only way to get a Guinea worm out of the skin safely is by wrapping it around a stick very ... very ... slowly, which can take up to a month!

HOW ARE MAGGOTS GOOD FOR YOU?

Some maggots love to munch away at dead flesh! They leave healthy flesh alone, though, and this can be put to good use with "maggot therapy," where maggots are applied to wounds to help keep them clean as they heal.

DID YOU KNOW?

New York City had a bedbug epidemic in 2007, when a record 6,889 calls were made to pest control companies. The tiny brown pests infested top hotels, hospitals, and schools, as well as homes.

CAN WORMS GET IN YOUR EYEBALLS?

Horseflies in West Africa spread the loa loa worm through their bites. The infection is also known as African eye worm, since the sufferer may feel the worms wriggling across their eyeballs. Eek!

WHY SHOULD YOU NOT PET CATERPILLARS?

Fluffy puss caterpillars look good enough to pet, but poisonous spines are lurking under their soft hair. When touched, the spines lodge painfully in the skin, causing numbness, blisters, and a rash.

DID YOU KNOW?

Biologist Mike Leahy is so committed to his work that he volunteered to swallow a tapeworm for research purposes. By the time he got rid of it, the worm was 3 m (10 ft) long!

WHAT IS SNAKE FLOSSING?

A man known as Snake Manu loves a bit of "snake flossing"—he puts slim snakes, including deadly cobras, up his nose and passes them out through his mouth.

DID YOU KNOW?

Head lice are sensitive to heat and will abandon the head of someone with a fever.

WHY ARE TICKS HARD TO REMOVE?

Ticks plunge barbs into the skin of their host to keep them anchored in place. That's why they're so difficult to remove!

WHAT HAPPENS IF LICE DRINK TOO MUCH?

Greedy young head lice can die from overfeeding, since their tiny guts spring a leak if they drink too much of your blood.

WHY SHOULD YOU WATCH WHERE YOU GO SWIMMING?

Bilharzia is a flatworm infection that can be caught by paddling or swimming in tropical lakes. It can damage the stomach, bladder, and liver, so think carefully next time you're tempted to go for a swim on vacation!

CAN HEAD LICE JUMP?

Head lice have little stumpy legs, so they can't jump. They don't walk very well on flat surfaces, either, so if one drops out of your hair, it is easy to catch!

ARE SWEAT BEES SWEATY?

No. Sweat bees are so-called because they love the salt in your sweat! Don't worry—their sting is almost painless compared to that of other bees.

DID YOU KNOW?

More than a billion people have a hookworm infection, which means they have tiny bloodsucking worms living in their intestines. Altogether, those hookworms suck a total of 10 million L (22 million pt) of blood a day!

WHICH INFECTION GIVES YOU BAD BURPS?

One nasty symptom of giardiasis is foul burps that can be so bad they induce vomiting! The infection is caused by a parasite with tentacle-like limbs.

WHY SHOULD YOU AVOID EMPTY BIRD NESTS?

If you find an empty bird nest, leave it alone. It could contain bird mites—and in spite of their name, these creatures are not fussy about drinking human blood!

DID YOU KNOW?

Cellulitis is a skin reaction that can follow an insect bite. The area around the bite swells alarmingly and has to be treated with antibiotics.

HOW TINY ARE THREADWORM EGGS?

Threadworm eggs are so small that you can't see them. They can float through the air, so you can catch worms if the eggs zoom up your nose when you breathe in!

ARE LEECHES EASY TO REMOVE?

Some leeches just won't let go! One Hong Kong woman had to have one surgically removed from her nostril, when it clung on for weeks after she washed her face in an infested stream. The nose invader was 5 cm (2 in) long.

DID YOU HEAR ABOUT THE GUY WHO TOOK HIS SNAKE TO A BANK?

In 2004, a South African man purposely released deadly puff adders into the bank that repossessed his car. A cleaner was bitten, and the man was charged with attempted murder.

DID YOU KNOW?

The bite of a fire ant feels like a nasty burn on your skin and turns into an itchy white blister.

HOW LONG IS LUNCH FOR A LEECH?

It takes 20 minutes for a leech to fill itself up with blood. Leeches secrete an enzyme that keeps blood from clotting as they feed. They usually drop off once they're full, but the bite continues bleeding until the clot-stopping substance has been washed away.

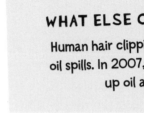

WHAT ELSE CAN HUMAN HAIR BE USED FOR?

Human hair clippings have also been used to help contain oil spills. In 2007, mats woven from hair were used to soak up oil at San Francisco's Ocean Beach.

DID YOU KNOW?

Australian rugby player Jamie Ainscough suffered a severe arm infection that puzzled doctors. The mystery was solved when an X-ray revealed an opponent's tooth stuck under his skin!

ARE HAIR CLIPPINGS USEFUL?

American barber Bill Black saved the hair clippings swept up from his floor and used them to make vests, shirts, ties, and even a bikini! Sounds itchy!

WHO HAS AN EAR ON HIS ARM?

Australian performance artist Stelarc had a human ear grafted onto his forearm in the name of art. He can literally turn a deaf ear to anyone who annoys him!

WHICH FISHERMAN BECAME BAIT?

Peter Hodge—from Britain—was a keen angler and wanted to be fed to the fish when he died. His ashes were mixed with fish food and thrown into the Huntspill River.

DID YOU KNOW?

Reclusive billionaire Howard Hughes had such a phobia of germs that his staff had to cover his cutlery handles with layers of tissue paper and cellophane.

WHO HAS THE BAGGIEST EARLOBES?

Hawaiian Kala Kaiwi used wooden disks to stretch the holes in his earlobes to an eye-watering 10 cm (4 in) across.

WHO PLAYS TUNES WITH HIS BOTTOM?

British entertainer Mr. Methane describes himself as "the world's only full-time performing flatulist." Yep, people pay to hear him fart tunes!

WHY SHOULD YOU ALWAYS CHECK A DENTIST'S QUALIFICATIONS?

When Italian police investigated complaints against dentist-from-hell Alvaro Perez, they discovered he had been using a regular power drill on his patients and had no dental qualifications at all.

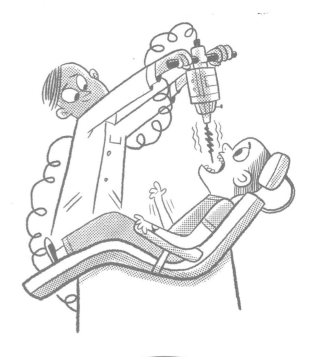

WHO LEFT MORE THAN FINGERPRINTS AT A CRIME SCENE?

A Swiss thief whose finger was cut off by broken glass was caught when police found the finger at the crime scene and matched its print with their records.

DID YOU KNOW?

Some African cultures engage in scarification, when patterns of raised scars are made on the skin as decoration or to show bravery.

WHO IS KING OF THE BIG MAC?

American burger enthusiast Don Gorske gobbled up 23,000 Big Macs in 36 years. He even has the receipts to prove it!

WHEN WAS A HEDGEHOG A WEAPON?

New Zealander William Singalargh was arrested for using a hedgehog as an offensive weapon—he threw it at a youth, causing scratches and puncture wounds.

DID YOU KNOW?

After spending five days with his arm trapped under a fallen boulder, mountaineer Aron Ralston had to take drastic action—he cut off his arm with a penknife. His bravery has been immortalized in the movie 127 Hours.

WHY SHOULDN'T YOU BITE YOUR NAILS?

British man Richard Ross was holding a nail (not a fingernail, a metal one!) between his lips while doing DIY, when he inhaled it! His ribs had to be broken to remove it.

WHAT HAPPENS TO YOUR BODY ON A ROLLER COASTER?

If you feel like your stomach has dropped when you're on a roller coaster, it's because it has! Your body reacts to the g-force on a roller coaster, meaning that your insides actually move around.

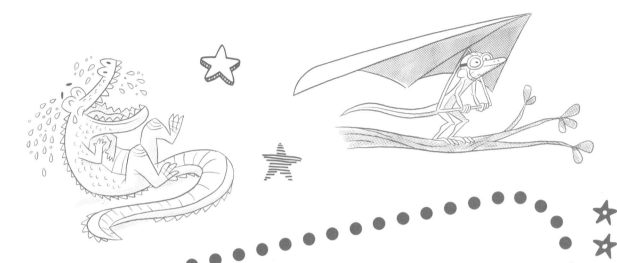

AWESOME
ANIMALS

DID YOU KNOW?

There are around 375 species of sharks. They live in all the world's oceans, from icy polar waters to warm, tropical seas. They also live at all levels of the ocean, from the shallows to the deep.

HOW MANY TEETH DO SHARKS GROW IN A LIFETIME?

Sharks' teeth are replaced every couple of weeks, so they are always in peak condition. They are arranged in rows in the mouth. As one tooth or row of teeth falls out, new ones move forward to take their place. Over their lifetime, sharks may grow and use over 20,000 teeth!

ARE SHARKS SMOOTH?

A shark's skin looks smooth—but if you stroked it the wrong way, it would feel like sandpaper. It is covered by tiny overlapping scales called dermal denticles, which reduce drag. Throughout the shark's life, old denticles drop off and are replaced by new ones.

DO SHARKS NEVER SLEEP?

Sharks never fall deeply asleep like humans. They need to keep swimming all the time to move water through their gills. They have "resting times," though, when they let one-half of their brain switch off.

HOW DO BUBBLES HELP WHALES HUNT?

Some whales trap their prey by blowing bubbles around them. The creatures can't swim through the little pockets of air and get stuck in the "bubble net."

DID YOU KNOW?

The bowhead whale, a type of whale found in the Arctic, can live for more than 200 years.

DO WHALES HAVE MELONS ON THEIR HEADS?

Toothed whales have a round mass of tissue on their foreheads called a "melon." They use these for echolocation, mapping a picture of the ocean around them using sound waves to track and locate their prey.

HOW BIG IS A BLUE WHALE?

The blue whale isn't just the biggest animal on Earth right now, it's the biggest animal ever recorded! They are 25-30 m (82-98 ft) long, weigh about 180 tonnes (198 tons), and their tongue weighs as much as a female elephant.

DO WE KNOW A LOT ABOUT THE DEEP OCEAN?

Humans have barely begun exploring the deep ocean. In fact, scientists think that we've only discovered 9 percent of all the species that live underwater.

ARE THERE FISH THAT CAN GLOW IN THE DARK?

In the deepest parts of the ocean, almost no light is able to filter down from the surface, so the creatures that live there have to make their own light. They do this using a process called bioluminescence, which allows them to glow in the dark to attract mates, lure prey, and spot predators.

DID YOU KNOW?

Despite appearances, dolphins are actually mammals. They give birth to live young, have body hair, and need to come to the surface to breathe.

HOW SMART ARE DOLPHINS?

Very! Dolphins are among the most intelligent creatures in the world. They have a complex "language," communicating through a series of clicks, squeaks, and growls. They have also been seen to use tools and solve puzzles.

WHAT IS THE SHARK'S TOP FIN FOR?

In scary movies, a dorsal fin poking above the surface warns us that a shark is coming. In reality, the dorsal fin acts like a stabilizer and stops the shark from rolling in the water.

WHY CAN'T FISH CHEW?

If fish chewed their food, it would interfere with the passage of water over their gills, and they would suffocate. Instead, some fish, such as sharks, swallow their food whole, while others have toothlike grinding mills in their throats that break the food down.

WHY DON'T SHARKS SINK?

The flow of water over a shark's pectoral (side) and pelvic (bottom) fins produces lift—just like air flowing over a plane's wing. This keeps sharks from sinking. Sharks change direction by tilting their fins.

DO WHALES HAVE FEET?

Not exactly, but they used to! Their bone structure shows traces of pelvises, and some are occasionally born with hints of hind limbs. Scientists believe that whales are evolved from prehistoric wolflike land mammals and may even have had hooves like horses.

WHAT'S A FEEDING FRENZY?

Once a group of sharks finds lots of prey, the blood in the water and the jerky movements of the fish overexcite the sharks. They might lunge at each other as well as the prey!

WHY DID THE CRAB CROSS THE ROAD?

Every year, Christmas Island red crabs travel across Christmas Island in the Indian Ocean in their thousands to breed. To keep them safe while they make their journey, locals have even built special crab bridges across roads to prevent them from being killed by passing cars.

DID YOU KNOW?

Green turtles migrate over 2,200 km (1,400 mi) across the ocean to lay their eggs.

DID YOU KNOW?

Jellyfish are 95 percent water, with the remaining 5 percent made up of muscles, nerves, and structural proteins.

HOW OLD ARE OCTOPUSES?

The oldest octopus fossil ever discovered is from the Carboniferous period about 296 million years ago—that's 50 million years before the first dinosaurs showed up.

WHAT IS A MERMAID'S PURSE?

About a third of sharks lay eggs in the water. The egg cases harden in the water and protect the growing embryo for two to 15 months. Then, the pup swims out of the case. Washed-up cases are nicknamed "mermaids' purses."

WHAT CAN A SHARK DO WITH A SAW?

Saw sharks are extremely rare. They have wide, flat bodies, but their distinguishing feature is a long, narrow snout studded with pointed teeth. The sharks use this "saw" to slash at fish or to probe the seabed for shellfish.

HOW DO REPTILES STAY WARM?

Reptiles are cold-blooded, which means that they have to use external sources to stay warm. Many lizards who live in hot areas will bask in the sun to warm up their skin.

DID YOU KNOW?

Blind snakes live underground and use other senses to find food: termites and ant eggs. Blind snakes can wolf down 100 ant eggs a minute!

CAN SNAKES DETECT HEAT?

Pythons, boas, and pit vipers have heat pits around their mouths that allow them to detect warm-blooded prey. Pit vipers' brains can turn the information from the pits into an image, so they "see" a thermogram (heat picture) of their prey.

WHY DO REPTILES STICK OUT THEIR TONGUES?

Many reptiles, including lizards and snakes, use their flickering tongues both to taste and smell. Their tongues pick up chemicals from the air, then wipe them onto two pits on the roof of the mouth. Those pits are a sense organ named Jacobson's organ.

WHICH IS THE STRONGEST SNAKE?

The green anaconda may be the most powerful constrictor. It squeezes with a force of 41 kg (90 lb) per 6.5 sq cm (1 sq in).

CAN GECKOS FLY?

They can't fly, but some of them can glide. The flying gecko has flaps of skin on its feet, which it uses like a parachute to glide up to 60 m (197 ft) between trees.

DID YOU KNOW?

Some snakes wiggle their tails, luring prey to come within striking distance. The prey thinks the tail is a smaller animal, such as a worm. Sidewinders and eyelash vipers do this.

WHAT GRUESOME SURVIVAL SKILL DO LIZARDS HAVE?

Many lizards can detach their tails from their bodies if they get caught by a hungry predator. Even after it's detached, the tail will continue to thrash about, distracting the predator and allowing the lizard to run away.

HOW DO KOMODO DRAGONS HUNT?

At first glance, Komodo dragons aren't the best hunters. They will ambush and attack other animals, including monkeys, deer, and wild boar, but rarely manage to kill their prey on the spot. Instead, the venom and bacteria from their saliva will gradually kill the animal over several days. Then, the Komodo dragon will use its powerful sense of smell to track down and eat the body.

HOW DOES A VENOMOUS SNAKE ATTACK?

When a venomous snake strikes, it sinks its fangs into its prey. Like a pair of deadly syringes, they pump venom into the victim's flesh. Vipers' fangs are so long that they have to fold back flat when they're not being used.

DO COBRAS SPIT?

Some snakes use venom to defend themselves. If a predator comes within 3 m (10 ft) of a spitting cobra, it may be sprayed with venom. The venom squirts from the cobra's fangs. If it gets in an attacker's eyes, it can cause blindness.

HOW STRONG IS AN ALLIGATOR'S STOMACH?

Alligators don't chew their food well, instead swallowing it in big chunks. Their stomach acid is so strong that it can fully dissolve most prey in two to three days. It can even dissolve bone—though this usually takes longer.

HOW DO YOU TELL THE DIFFERENCE BETWEEN A CROCODILE AND AN ALLIGATOR?

There are a few ways to tell the difference between these scaly reptiles. Alligators have rounded snouts, and you cannot see their teeth when their mouths are closed. Crocodiles, on the other hand, have pointed snouts and teeth that stick out when their mouths are open.

DID ALLIGATORS EAT DINOSAURS?

Fossils found of Deinosuchus, a 12 m (39 ft) alligator that lived around 70-80 million years ago, had dinosaur bones in the stomach. This suggests that even dinosaurs weren't safe from this enormous reptile!

WHAT ARE CROCODILE TEARS?

When a crocodile eats too quickly, it swallows a lot of air, which triggers its tear-producing lachrimal glands, making it look like the croc is crying. The term *crocodile tears* is sometimes used to describe fake or insincere tears.

CAN SNAKES FLY?

The paradise flying snake lives in rain forests. It cannot really fly like a bird, but it can glide up to 100 m (328 ft) from tree to tree. It sucks in its underside and stretches out its ribs, shaping its body like a simple wing.

HOW BIG IS THE BIGGEST REPTILE?

The biggest reptile is the saltwater crocodile, which can grow to up to 5 m (18 ft) long. By comparison, the teeny nano chameleon is only 13.5 mm (0.5 in) long.

DID YOU KNOW?

Some desert reptiles have a second bladder that they can use to store water for months at a time.

WHAT HAPPENS WHEN LIZARDS GET COLD?

Because they're cold-blooded, reptiles don't feel temperature like we do. When lizards get cold, they slow down. When the temperature drops too much, the heat-loving green iguana will freeze completely, and it won't start moving again until it warms up.

57

DID YOU KNOW?

The gavial, a kind of crocodile from India, has over 100 teeth.

HOW DO YOU STOP A GILA MONSTER?

The Gila monster is a lizard from South America and Mexico. Although it's only about 0.5 m (2 ft) long, its bite is so strong that the only way to detach one that's bitten you is to drown it.

ARE KOMODO DRAGONS POISONOUS?

Komodo dragons are lizards that are 3 m (10 ft) long. They aren't poisonous, but there are so many bacteria in their mouths—growing in rotten meat between their teeth—that a bite from one often leads to blood poisoning and death. Baby Komodo dragons will eat their brothers and sisters if they are hungry and there is no other food.

WHAT MAKES THE RATTLE ON A RATTLESNAKE?

The rattle on a rattlesnake's tail is made of rings of dead skin. It builds up as the snake grows older, so the louder the rattle, the larger the snake.

DO CROCODILES CHEW?

Crocodiles can't bite and chew. Instead, they hold their prey underwater to drown it, then twist their bodies around to tear chunks off the victim.

WERE THERE REALLY CROCODILES AT THE TIME OF THE DINOSAURS?

Over 100 million years ago, crocodiles were twice the size they are now—up to 12 m (40 ft) long—and they could eat dinosaurs.

HOW LONG IS A CHAMELEON'S TONGUE?

A chameleon's tongue can be twice as long as its body and must be kept curled up to fit inside its mouth. The end of its tongue can have a club-like lump oiled with sticky goo, which helps it catch insects.

DID YOU KNOW?

The horned lizard from South America shoots blood out of its eyes when it's attacked. It increases the blood pressure in its sinuses until they explode, spraying blood onto the attacker.

WHY DO SNAKES SHED THEIR SKIN?

A snake's long, limbless body is covered in scaly snakeskin. As it grows, it becomes too big for its skin and needs to shed it. Unlike humans, who lose old skin cells each day, the snake sheds its entire skin at one time.

HOW CAN YOU TELL WHETHER A TURTLE IS A BOY OR A GIRL?

The temperature an egg is kept at before it hatches determines the sex of the turtle. If the eggs are warm, the hatchlings will be female, and if they're cooler, they'll be male.

DID YOU KNOW?

Newborn rattlesnakes have no rattle! The bead needed to make the rattle noise in their tail does not form until they have shed their first skin.

WHY DO ALLIGATORS MAKE THE BEST MOTHERS?

Alligator mothers carry their babies in their mouths to keep them safe and warm.

HOW DO CATS CARE FOR THEIR CLAWS?

Cats' claws are sheathed in a protective covering, so that walking does not blunt them. When cats scrape their claws down a tree trunk, they are scratching away the worn, outer layers to reveal new, sharp tips.

DID YOU KNOW?

Cats do not always kill prey completely. You might see a cat batting a mouse to and fro. This act may look cruel, but it is just the cat's way of checking to make sure the mouse is no longer able to escape.

HOW DO CATS HUNT?

Cats creep up on their prey, keeping low to the ground. Just before they pounce, they check their balance with a wiggle of their bottom. They grip the victim with their claws and deliver a killer bite to the neck.

WHY DOES MY CAT BRING IN LIVE MICE?

Mother cats bring their kittens live prey so that they can rehearse hunting. Your pet might be trying to teach another cat in the household— or it might be trying to teach you!

WHO CAN TASTE BETTER—ME OR MY CAT?

Experts used to think cats could only detect meaty and fatty tastes. Now we know that their sense of taste is more complex. Still, cats have fewer than 475 taste buds, whereas humans have around 9,000!

WHY CAN'T PET CATS ROAR?

Only lions, tigers, leopards, and jaguars can roar. These big cats have a special larynx (voice box) and a flexible throat bone that work together to create the roar.

DID YOU KNOW?

Cats have whiskers on their face and wrists. Whiskers sense movements in the air, allowing cats to form a picture of their surroundings. They help cats avoid obstacles and pinpoint their prey.

WHY MIGHT A CAT PURR AT THE VET'S?

When cats purr in anxious situations, they are not expressing contentment. They are trying to reassure themselves. Perhaps the sound helps them feel safe because it reminds them of being a kitten.

DO CATS HAVE A GOOD SENSE OF SMELL?

Cats' sense of smell is 14 times better than humans'. However, unlike dogs, cats do not track prey by smell. A special organ on the roof of the cat's mouth picks up scents. Sometimes they gape (open their mouths wide) to smell better.

HOW GOOD IS A CAT'S HEARING?

Cats' ears are large and able to move. They can turn toward a sound and figure out where it is coming from. Cats can hear high-pitched sounds, such as mouse squeaks, outside the range of human hearing.

DID YOU KNOW?

A cat's nose has a unique print, just as your fingerprints do!

HOW DO CATS SAY HELLO?

Cats say "hello" with a warbling sound, sometimes called a "chirrup." They make this friendly noise to greet other cats. They also chirrup to their owners—the sound means "Welcome home!" or "I'm back!"

WHAT'S THAT HORRIBLE NOISE CATS MAKE AT NIGHT?

Caterwauling is the nasty, screeching sound that cats sometimes make. Females do it to tell toms (males) who live nearby that they are ready to mate. Cats also howl if they are anxious, in pain, or simply want attention.

HOW DO YOU KNOW IF A CAT IS AFRAID?

An angry cat will send warning signals before biting or scratching. To warn others to steer clear, the cat draws back its ears, narrows its eyes, and bares its teeth. Fearful cats flatten their ears, too, but they widen their eyes.

DID YOU KNOW?

When a cat is annoyed, it swishes its tail to and fro. This, like growling, is the cat's way of saying "Go away!" When a cat is really afraid, it puffs out its tail and fur, so that its body looks bigger than it really is.

HOW CAN I TELL IF MY CAT WANTS TO PLAY?

Even fully grown cats can be kittenish and playful. Trail a piece of ribbon past the nose of a relaxed, sprawling cat. If its eyes open and its ears and whiskers perk up, it wants to play.

WHY DO CATS CLIMB?

Leopards, jaguars, and many other wild cats are at ease in the trees. Pet cats enjoy the safety of a treetop lookout, too. Climbing a tree trunk does not take too much effort, thanks to their light body and strong claws for gripping.

DO CATS DREAM?

Cats spend two-thirds of their lives asleep. Like sleeping humans, they have different cycles of brain activity, including REM sleep, when dreaming occurs. Dreaming cats twitch and even swat imaginary prey!

WHY DON'T CATS FALL OFF FENCES?

Cats can walk along the narrowest ledges and fences. They rehearse their tightrope skills as kittens. If they fall, they almost always land on their feet. A balance organ in their ears helps them steady themselves in midair.

WHY ARE CATS SO FLEXIBLE?

Like humans, cats have a backbone made up of vertebrae (smaller bones). Their bones are only loosely connected, so the spine is very flexible. Cats do not have a fixed collarbone under the neck, so the front legs are free to stretch forward.

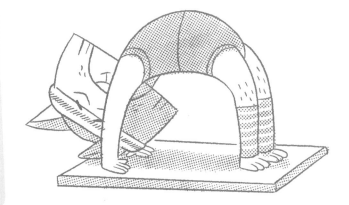

CAN KITTENS SEE WHEN THEY ARE BORN?

Kittens are born with their eyes and ears closed. Their main sense is smell. The kittens' eyes open a week or two later, but it takes a few days before they can focus. Kittens start to hear at two to three weeks old.

WHY DO CATS NEED DRY FOOD?

Most cats eat a combination of wet food from cans and pouches, and dry food. The dry food helps to keep their teeth clean and their gums healthy. Cats enjoy fresh fish and meat, too.

DO CATS NEED TO GROOM?

Cats are constantly grooming. They run their rough, comblike tongue through their hairs to keep them clean and sleek. Cats use a licked paw as a washcloth to groom harder-to-reach places, such as the top of the head.

ARE DOGS GOOD DETECTIVES?

Absolutely! Dogs are great at tracking, so we use them to find missing people. They can pick up the "trail" scent of someone lost or a criminal on the run, even when it is days old. Dogs also help find survivors after disasters.

WHY DO DOGS HAVE WHISKERS?

Dogs have whiskers around their muzzle and above their jaw. These feelers help dogs with their sense of touch and their "spatial awareness"—for instance, being able to tell if they can fit through a narrow gap in a fence.

WHY DO DOGS HAVE GREAT NIGHT SIGHT?

Cones are the parts of the eye's retina that sense color and detail. Dogs have 10 times fewer cones than we do, and they see the world in only blues and yellows. However, their retinas have more rods than ours. Rods are the parts of the retina that see the best in dim light.

DO DOG WHISTLES REALLY WORK?

Yes! Dog whistles produce a sound that dogs can hear but humans can't. Dogs can hear twice the range of frequencies that humans can. They are better at hearing across distances, too—four times better than us!

WHICH DOGS ARE BEST FOR HERDING?

Some dogs have been bred to help farmers look after their livestock. Collies, sheepdogs, cattle dogs, and mountain dogs all have a keen herding instinct and are intelligent, too. They can control sheep, goats, or even cattle.

DO DOGS GO ON TRIAL?

At sheepdog trials, herding dogs can show off their skills. The exact challenges vary, but usually the dogs must drive the sheep around an obstacle course and into a pen, and also separate one or more animals from the rest.

WHICH DOG IS THE FASTEST?

The fastest dogs—greyhounds and salukis— were bred to catch rabbits and hares. If they spot one, they cannot resist chasing it! They can race along at 64 km/h (40 mph). Most dogs are built for staying power, not speed, however.

WHY DOES MY DOG LICK MY FACE?

Pups lick their mothers' faces to prompt them to regurgitate food, which the pups can eat. Dogs do the same to their owners, who are a little like parents to them. They know their owners won't regurgitate food, though!

WHAT DO DOGS' TAILS TELL YOU?

Dogs' tails are very expressive. Dogs wag them enthusiastically when they are feeling friendly and contented. Dogs that are doing things they enjoy, such as running or playing games, usually hold their tails upright.

DID YOU KNOW?

Dogs mark their territory with urine or poop. Sometimes they scrape at the ground near the scent message. The claw marks help draw the attention of other dogs to the smelly marker.

WHY DO DOGS HOWL LIKE WOLVES?

Wolves howl to communicate with each other across long distances. The pack can keep track of each other, and it can also communicate with other packs. Pet dogs howl to express worry or anxiety, for instance, if their owners are away.

IS IT OK TO FEED MY DOG BETWEEN MEALS?

Obesity is a common problem for dogs—more than 50 percent of dogs in the United States are obese. Limiting food to mealtimes makes it easier to stop dogs from overeating.

DID YOU KNOW?

Dogs are carnivores, or meat-eaters. They like nothing better than gnawing meat off a bone. Pet dogs get most of their meat from canned food, which also contains cereals. Crunchy kibble keep their teeth and gums healthy.

HOW GOOD IS A DOG'S SENSE OF TASTE?

Dogs have only 1,700 taste buds, compared to a human's 9,000. Most are at the tip of the tongue. Dogs distinguish between bitter, sweet, salty, and sour—and like us, some dogs have a very sweet tooth!

WHY DOES MY DOG CHEW?

Puppies chew to explore the world and soothe their itchy gums when they're teething. Adult dogs chew because they like it! Giving pets toys made of hard rubber or rawhide will keep them from chewing your belongings.

CAN DOGS HAVE JOBS?

Dogs make great helpers. Some are trained to assist people who are blind, deaf, or in a wheelchair. Their amazing ability to smell chemical changes means that dogs can even forewarn owners with epilepsy when they are about to have a seizure.

CAN PUPPIES SEE AT BIRTH?

At first, puppies just sleep and feed. They whimper and jostle for position. Their eyes and ears are sealed for the first three weeks. The only sense the pups need is smell—so they can sniff out their mother's milk.

DID YOU KNOW?

A dog that is always scratching may have fleas. A vet can advise on the best way to prevent fleas. Other parasites that can affect dogs include ticks (picked up on walks) and worms.

DO YOU NEED TO BRUSH A PET DOG REGULARLY?

Although dogs groom themselves, they also need help from their owners. Regular brushing helps to keep coats sleek and strengthens the bond between owner and dog. Sometimes dogs will need bathing, too.

71

WHAT DO PUPPIES EAT?

For the first three or four weeks, puppies only need milk. Then they can start to try solid food, such as puppy kibble mixed with water. They continue drinking their mother's milk, though, until they are weaned at six to eight weeks old.

WHAT TEMPERATURE CAN HUSKIES WORK IN?

Siberian huskies can live and work in temperatures as low as -51 °C (-60 °F).

ARE MOST DALMATIANS GOOD LISTENERS?

Actually, Dalmatians are genetically disposed toward deafness. Until this was discovered, they were thought not to listen to their owners!

DID YOU KNOW?

Basenji dogs have unusually shaped larynxes and do not bark—they make a yodeling sound!

HOW LONG IS A WOODPECKER'S TONGUE?

A woodpecker's tongue can be a third of its body length! It has a barb on the end of it for skewering grubs. Yummy!

HOW LONG HAVE INSECTS EXISTED?

Winged insects first appeared about 300 million years ago, even farther back in time than dinosaurs.

DID YOU KNOW?

Osedax mucofloris is a slimy sea worm that feeds on whale remains and looks like a flower growing from the bone it's eating. Its name means "bone-eating mucus flower"!

WHICH SEA CREATURE IS A COPYCAT?

The mimic octopus can change its shape and the shade of its skin to look like other sea creatures. It can even make itself long and thin to do an impression of a sea snake!

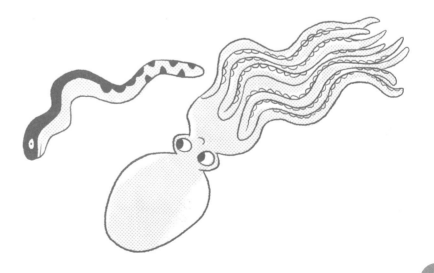

HOW DO BEAVERS SEE UNDERWATER?

Beavers have a set of transparent eyelids to protect their eyes as they swim underwater.

WHICH SEA CREATURE JOINED THE ARMY?

The United States and Russian armies have trained dolphins to rescue lost divers and seek out underwater mines.

DID YOU KNOW?

It can take a month for the contents of a sloth's stomach to digest completely.

WHICH ANIMAL IS NOT SCARED OF SCORPIONS?

Meerkats are immune to many deadly venoms and will eat scorpions ... stinger and all!

ARE ELEPHANTS LEFT-HANDED?

Of course not. But in the same way that people are right- or left-handed, elephants are right- or left-tusked!

CAN FISH WALK?

Some fish can! Mudskippers can survive on land and have strong fins that they use as legs to get around.

DID YOU KNOW?

Chemicals taken from Kamchatka crabs have been used to treat burns.

HOW MANY ANTS DOES AN ANTEATER EAT?

A giant anteater gobbles up around 30,000 ants and termites in one day, using its sticky tongue, which can be as long as 61 cm (2 ft)!

DO POLAR BEARS HAVE WHITE FUR?

Nope! Polar bears' hollow hair is actually transparent. It looks white because of the way it scatters light.

CAN DOLPHINS HAVE RUBBER TAILS?

Fuji the dolphin put on weight after having her diseased tail amputated because she couldn't swim properly. Handlers at the Japanese aquarium came up with a speedy solution—a new tail made from a tough rubber used in Formula One race cars!

DID YOU KNOW?

Birds can eat berries that are highly poisonous to humans.

WHERE DOES A BURROWING OWL MAKE ITS HOME?

The burrowing owl makes its nest underground and lines it with shredded cow dung.

DO AARDVARKS EAT FRUIT?

The only fruit eaten by aardvarks is known as the aardvark cucumber. African indigenous people call it aardvark dung!

CAN BATS FISH?

The greater bulldog bat likes to go fishing! Its super sonar detects the slightest of ripples ... then it swoops down to catch the fish in its sharp wing claws!

DID YOU KNOW?

Frogs do not drink water; they absorb it through their skin.

WHICH IS HEAVIER— HUMANS OR ANTS?

The total combined weight of the world's ant population is about the same as the weight of the human population.

CAN AN OWL READ A BOOK?

Owls are farsighted, so they cannot clearly see things close up.

CAN ELEPHANTS CONTROL THEIR TUMMY RUMBLES?

An elephant's tummy makes lots of noise when it's digesting food, so elephants can stop their digestion at will if there's any danger of a predator hearing it!

CAN ARMADILLOS DIVE?

An armadillo can stay underwater for up to six minutes! First, it fills its stomach with air; otherwise it would sink under the weight of its heavy plating.

DID YOU KNOW?

Staff at a British zoo had to hand-feed milk to a baby colobus monkey after it was rejected by its mother ... for having the hiccups!

IS THERE A FLAT TORTOISE?

The African pancake tortoise has a flat, soft shell ... just like a pancake! The shell is no use against predators, but it does help the tortoise avoid them by enabling it to hide in narrow crevices.

WHAT DO GIANT CATFISH EAT?

A giant catfish frightened divers at a Dutch vacation park. The monster fish was found to be 2.3 m (7 ft 6 in) long and ate three ducks a day, but staff promised that it wouldn't eat people!

HOW DO PYGMY MICE FIND WATER?

The African pygmy mouse gets water by stacking pebbles in front of its burrow and drinking the dew from them in the morning.

CAN PIGS SWEAT?

No. They roll about in mud to keep cool in hot weather!

DID YOU KNOW?

Both the coat and the skin of a tiger have stripes.

DO SPIDERS GET CROSS?

The St. Andrew's Cross spider is so-called because it rests in its web with its legs outstretched in an "X" shape.

CAN BIRDS MOVE THEIR EYES?

Birds' eyes are fixed in their sockets, so they have to move their whole head to look at something—try it yourself, keeping your eyes still!

WHY ARE FLAMINGOS PINK?

The pink shade of a flamingo comes from all the shrimp it eats. A pale flamingo is one that's not getting enough food!

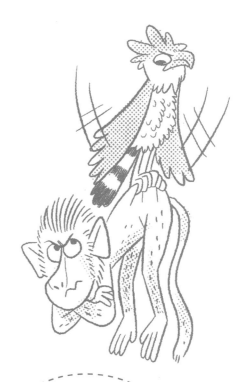

CAN AN EAGLE LIFT A MONKEY?

The harpy eagle is so large and powerful that it can easily carry away a monkey in its talons.

DID YOU KNOW?

A German farmer found a novel way of protecting his sheep from hoof infection. He dressed his flock in special little boots!

HOW MANY TEETH DO ELEPHANTS HAVE?

Elephants have only four teeth, which can be replaced up to six times in their lifetime.

CAN A TAPIR GRAB WITH ITS NOSE?

The tapir has a long snout that is prehensile—that means it can move in all directions and grasp things!

WHERE DID ALL THE SWANS GO?

An elderly Swedish woman took animal rescue a little too far. Police found that she had been sheltering 11 swans in her tiny Stockholm apartment for more than five years!

WHAT CAN SURVIVE WITHOUT WATER THE LONGEST—A CAMEL OR A RAT?

A kangaroo rat can go without water for longer than a camel.

CAN A FROG SURVIVE FROST?

A tiny tree frog wandered into the freezer of a cafeteria in Darwin, Australia, and was found frozen solid. Once it thawed out, it was fine.

ARE ALL PIRANHAS DANGEROUS?

There are approximately 20 different kinds of piranha fish, but only four of them are dangerous.

HOW LONG DOES A SNAIL SNOOZE?

Snails can sleep for three years.

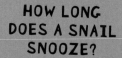

WHERE DO BATS LIVE IN WEBS?

Some West African bats are so tiny that they live in spiderwebs.

HOW DO YOU MAKE A FROG FALL ASLEEP?

Amphibian skin absorbs chemicals as well as water. So, a frog sitting in an anesthetic solution will quickly go to sleep.

DO SEA PIGS HAVE CURLY TAILS?

No! Sea pigs are a type of sea cucumber. They live in really deep oceans, rolling around in the mud on the seabed and eating it!

HOW MANY BEETLES CAN YOU FIT IN AN ELEPHANT POOP?

One pat of elephant dung can contain up to 7,000 dung beetles!

DID YOU KNOW?

Around 200 cats brought to a Chinese village to get rid of the rat problem were rewarded for their hard work with an enormous fish banquet!

WHY DO PANDAS SPEND AGES EATING?

Pandas cannot digest bamboo very well, but they still spend all day eating it—98 percent of what they eat is bamboo!

WHAT DOES A RIBBON WORM DO IF IT GETS HUNGRY?

If it has no food, a ribbon worm can eat up to 95 percent of its own body to survive.

WHAT SEA CREATURE DARES TO ATTACK A WHALE?

Whales have been found with circular scars on their skin—marks from the suckers of giant squid.

WHICH CRAB CAN'T SWIM?

The coconut crab, or robber crab, lives on land and will drown in water.

DID YOU KNOW?

Giant clamshells are so big that in the past, they have been used as children's bathtubs and baptismal fonts.

CAN OWLS TURN THEIR HEADS IN A CIRCLE?

Owls cannot turn their heads the whole way around. They can turn them farther than you can, though—to an angle of 135 degrees in each direction.

554131216

CAN HORSES BECOME ALLERGIC TO HAY?

A horse in Coventry, England, was found to have hay fever! Teddy the horse's owner had to give him shredded newspaper to sleep on instead.

WHY WAS A COW ARRESTED?

A cow caused an accident by wandering into a road in Columbia and was punished by being put into prison.

DID YOU KNOW?

Penguins have a filter above their eyes that converts salt water to fresh water. The excess brine drips out of their bills, and sometimes they sneeze it out!

HOW BIG ARE THE BIGGEST SEA STARS?

Giant sea stars are starfish that can have an arm span of more than 60 cm (24 in)! They can be brown, green, red, or orange.

ARE TURTLES DANGEROUS?

Yes. The powerful jaws and sharp teeth of a snapping turtle can rip off a person's finger.

IS A TARANTULA HAWK A SPIDER OR A BIRD?

The tarantula hawk is actually a wasp! The female attacks and immobilizes a tarantula so she can lay her egg on its body. The hatched larva then eats the tarantula alive.

IS THERE REALLY A SEE-THROUGH FROG?

The glass frog has a transparent body—its blood vessels, stomach, and beating heart are all visible.

DID YOU KNOW?

The axolotl is a pale amphibian that is partway between a tadpole and a lizard and lives in a single lake in Mexico. Some axolotls change shape and become land creatures, but most don't ever change.

DO ALL MOSQUITOES BITE?

Only female mosquitoes bite and suck blood—they need the protein in blood, so that they can lay eggs. The males eat only nectar from flowers.

DO TOADS GET SICK?

When a toad is sick, it vomits up its own stomach, which hangs out of its mouth for a short time before it swallows it back down.

HOW TOUGH IS A SCORPION?

A scorpion can go for a whole year without eating. It can withstand extremes of temperature and even radiation. A scorpion could be frozen in a block of ice for three weeks and walk away unharmed. It can survive 200 times the dose of radiation that would kill a person!

HOW DO SPIDERS FEED?

Spiders inject flies and bugs with a chemical that paralyzes them and dissolves their insides. The spider then sucks out the liquid, since it can't chew. A spider that isn't hungry will wrap up extra bugs in its web to keep for later.

WHAT'S THE WORLD'S BIGGEST SPIDER?

Goliath birdeater spiders are the world's largest spider by mass. They can grow to the size of a dinner plate and kill small birds.

HOW MUCH BLOOD DOES A MOSQUITO DRINK?

A mosquito can drink one-and-a-half times its own weight in blood at a single meal.

HOW TOUGH ARE COCKROACHES?

A cockroach can withstand more than 120 times the force of Earth's gravity—an astronaut passes out at 12 times the pressure of gravity. A cockroach can also survive being frozen in a block of ice for two days and even live for a week after its head is cut off!

HOW FAST DO COCKROACHES BREED?

Cockroaches breed so fast that if all the young survived and reproduced, there would be 10 million cockroaches from a single pair by the end of a year.

DID YOU KNOW?

A single female fly can hatch up to 1,000 babies (maggots) in her lifetime.

HOW DO FLIES EAT?

Flies eat by vomiting up something they've eaten previously, so that the chemicals in their vomit can start to dissolve the new meal. When it's sloppy, they suck it all up again. That's why it's a really bad idea to eat anything a fly's been sitting on!

HOW MUCH BLOOD DOES A LEECH DRINK?

A leech will suck blood until it is 10 times its original size and can't hold any longer. Once it's full, it drops off its victim. Leeches don't only suck from the outside of your body, either. If you drink water with a leech in it, the leech can attach to the inside of your mouth or throat. In a river, leeches can go into your bottom and suck you from the inside. Some leeches have three mouths, with up to 100 teeth.

CAN YOU DIE FROM AN ANT STING?

The bulldog ant from Australia will sting again and again while holding on with its fierce jaws. It can kill a human in 15 minutes.

CAN ARMIES OF ANTS EAT LARGE PREY?

Driver ants and army ants both march in massive colonies and will strip to the bones any animal they come across. They'll even tackle a wounded crocodile or lion that can't get away. Driver ants slash at their victims, who eventually bleed to death from thousands of tiny cuts.

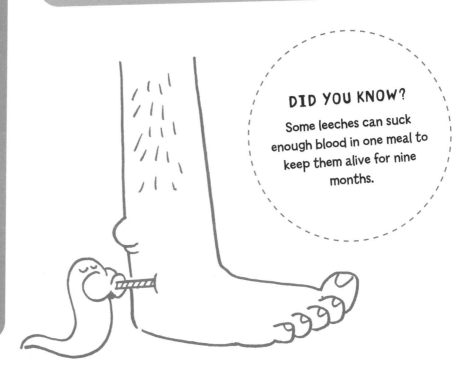

DID YOU KNOW?

Some leeches can suck enough blood in one meal to keep them alive for nine months.

HOW HIGH CAN A FLEA JUMP?

A flea can jump 30,000 times without stopping. It can jump up to 220 times its own body length—a flea the size of an adult human could jump over a 25-floor building and 0.4 km (more than a quarter of a mile) along the ground.

WHAT IS A PRAYING MANTIS?

A praying mantis is an insect something like a cricket but up to 12 cm (5 in) long. It can kill and eat small lizards and birds, holding them impaled on a special spike it has developed for the purpose. The female praying mantis begins to eat the male during mating; he keeps going, but she eventually eats all of him.

IF YOU CUT A WORM IN HALF, WILL IT GROW AGAIN?

A planarian worm will regrow its other half if cut in two. If two planarians are cut in half, they can be mixed up and reattach to the wrong half.

WHICH CATERPILLAR GROWS THE FASTEST?

The caterpillar of the polyphemus moth in North America eats 86,000 times its own birth weight in the first 56 days of its life. This is equal to a human baby eating nearly 270 metric tons (298 tons) of food!

DO ANY BUGS LAY THEIR EGGS ON DEAD ANIMALS?

When the Nicrophorus beetle finds a small dead animal, it pushes it into a suitable place, takes some of its fur to make a nest, and lays its eggs near the body. When the eggs hatch into maggots, they feed on the dead body.

DO TERMITES FART A LOT?

Termites fart out between 20 and 80 million metric tons of gas every year (not each—in total!).

WHAT ARE NOSE BOTS?

Nose bots are maggots that live inside the noses of animals that graze, such as sheep, cows, and horses.

WHAT ARE ZOMBIE WORMS?

Bone-eating zombie worms live on the decaying bodies of dead whales. They have no gut but bore deeply into the bones. Microbes inside the worms digest chemicals sucked out of the bones.

DID YOU KNOW?

Maggots are quite intelligent, and demonstrate group decision-making.

DAZZLING DINOSAURS

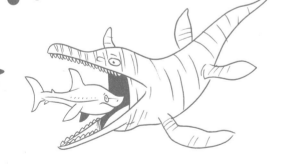

DID YOU KNOW?

Dinosaurs were different from other reptiles because their legs were positioned directly beneath them, rather than splayed out to the sides.

WHAT WERE THE DINOSAURS?

The dinosaurs were a group of land-dwelling reptiles that first appeared on Earth about 230 million years ago. There were hundreds of species of dinosaurs; some were gentle plant-eaters, while others were ferocious killers. After dominating the globe for 160 million years, the dinosaurs mysteriously died out around 65 million years ago.

WHAT'S INSIDE DINOSAUR DUNG?

Preserved dinosaur dung is called coprolite, and it reveals what dinosaurs were eating millions of years ago. Scientists have discovered pieces of bone, parts of plants, and fish scales inside dinosaur coprolite.

WHAT DOES "DINOSAUR" MEAN?

When the first dinosaur remains were unearthed in the nineteenth century, scientists were not sure what they had discovered. They named the owners of the huge fossilized bones "dinosaurs," which means "fearfully great lizards."

HOW DO WE KNOW ABOUT THE DINOSAURS?

We have learned everything we know about dinosaurs from the remains they left behind. These include fossilized bones and skeletons, footprints preserved in rock, and fossilized dinosaur dung. By studying these remains, scientists are able to establish what the dinosaurs looked like, how they moved, and what they ate.

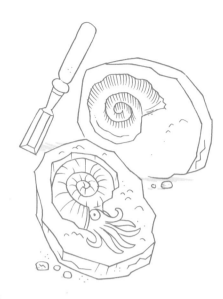

WHO DISCOVERED THE DINOSAURS?

The first dinosaur remains were discovered by accident in the English countryside. In 1822, Mary Ann Mantell and her husband, Dr. Gideon Mantell, found what looked like giant lizard teeth and several large bones buried in the ground. The couple continued to dig for more bones, until a fuller picture of the creature emerged.

DID YOU KNOW?

An ammonite is a common fossil of a shelled sea creature from the time of the dinosaurs.

WHAT IS A FOSSIL?

A fossil is the remains of an animal or plant that has been buried underground and preserved in rock. Fossils are mostly made up of the harder parts of an animal, such as its teeth or bones, rather than its softer body parts. Imprints such as footprints and feathers can also be fossilized. A fossil can be as small as a tooth or claw, or as large as a complete dinosaur skeleton.

WHICH DINOSAUR HAD BEEN FOUND?

After much research, Dr. Mantell concluded that the teeth and bones belonged to a reptile that resembled a giant iguana, He named this creature Iguanodon (ig-WAH-noh-don), which means "iguana tooth."

WHAT DID IGUANODON LOOK LIKE?

To begin with, Mantell thought that Iguanodon walked on four legs, had a spike on its nose, and dragged its tail along the ground. His theory changed after the remains of 40 Iguanodons were discovered in a Belgian mine in 1878. The skeletons were pieced together to show that Iguanodon walked on two legs, had a spike on its thumb instead of its nose, and kept its tail off the ground.

WERE ALL DINOSAURS RELATED?

There were hundreds of different species of dinosaurs, but all belonged to an ancient family named archosaurs, or "ruling reptiles." Modern crocodiles and birds also belong to this family—so did a range of strange and startling creatures that lived alongside the dinosaurs during the Mesozoic Era.

DID EORAPTOR EAT MEAT?

Around 1 m (3 ft) in length, Eoraptor (EE-oh-rap-tor) is often regarded as one of the earliest dinosaurs. Standing on two legs with two small arms, Eoraptor resembled the large predators that followed. However, there was one big difference. Eoraptor's jaw contained a combination of knifelike and leaflike teeth, meaning that it must have fed on both meat and plants to survive.

DID YOU KNOW?

The meat-eating dinosaurs were "bipedal," which means that they walked on two legs.

WHAT WERE THE FIRST DINOSAURS?

The first true dinosaurs were small meat-eaters, such as Eoraptor, that appeared in South America during the Late Triassic period. Measuring up to 2 m (6.5 ft) tall, these predators had curved finger claws, hollow limb bones for speed, and skulls that absorbed shock when biting prey. They would evolve into the large killer dinosaurs.

WHAT DID THE ANCESTORS OF DINOSAURS LOOK LIKE?

Euparkeria (yoo-PAR-kare-ee-uh) was one of the oldest-known archosaurs and an ancestor to the dinosaurs that followed. With scaly skin, a back covered in small, bumpy plates, and sharp, pointed teeth, Euparkeria walked on two legs and preyed upon small vertebrates.

WHEN DID THE DINOSAURS LIVE?

The dinosaurs lived, thrived, and died out during the Mesozoic Era, which lasted for 180 million years. The Mesozoic Era was broken into three shorter ages: the Triassic, Jurassic, and Cretaceous periods. The dinosaurs appeared around 230 million years ago during the Late Triassic period. By the end of the Cretaceous period, they were extinct.

DID PLATEOSAURUS WALK ON TWO FEET OR FOUR?

Plateosaurus (PLAT-ee-oh-SORE-us) was a Late Triassic period plant-eater that lived across the plains of Europe. A large number of fossilized skeletons, both adults and juveniles, have been found in modern-day Germany. Plateosaurus was a link between the two-footed meat-eating dinosaurs and the large four-footed plant-eaters. This is because Plateosaurus normally walked on four feet, but it could also stand on two feet to pick the leaves from treetops. It was the first dinosaur to be able to eat high vegetation; before it, plant-eaters were stumpy with a short neck, so they foraged nearer ground level.

WHAT WERE THE MAIN TYPES OF DINOSAURS?

Dinosaurs are divided into two main groups and are classified according to the shape of their hip bones. The two types of dinosaurs are saurischians, which means "lizard-hipped," and ornithischians, which means "bird-hipped."

DID YOU KNOW?

During the Triassic period, the Earth was spinning faster than it does today. Back then, one day was only 23 hours long.

WHAT WAS THE DINOSAUR WORLD LIKE?

The dinosaur world was one of continual change. Over millions of years, hundreds of different dinosaur species appeared and died out again, as the Earth underwent its own vast changes. During the time of the dinosaurs, every imaginable environment came and went: deserts, swamps, wetlands, forests, tundra, and open plains.

WHICH DINOSAURS PLUNDERED THE PLAINS?

The plains of the Late Cretaceous period were dominated by herds of plant-eating dinosaurs. These included the ceratopsians: horned and frilled dinosaurs such as Centrosaurus (SEN-troh-sore-us), Styracosaurus (sty-RAK-oh-sore-us), and Chasmosaurus (KAZ-moh-sore-us). The ceratopsians were hunted by predators such as Albertosaurus (al-BERT-oh-sore-us).

WHO RULED THE FORESTS?

The forests of the Cretaceous period were home to some of the most ferocious dinosaurs, such as Tyrannosaurus rex (ty-RAN-oh-SORE-us REX) and Troodon (TROH-oh-don). They hunted plant-eaters such as Kritosaurus (KRIT-oh-sore-us), a duck-billed dinosaur that fed on low-lying shrubs. The forests were also the domain of the large plant-eaters, such as Diplodocus (DIP-loh-dock-us) and Stegosaurus (STEG-oh-sore-us).

WHICH REPTILES RULED THE SKIES?

While dinosaurs dominated the land during the Mesozoic Era, a different group of reptiles ruled the air. These flying predators were named pterosaurs, or "winged reptiles," and they were the terror of the skies. However, pterosaurs were not only confined to the air—they hunted land and sea creatures as well.

DID YOU KNOW?

Pterodactylus (TEH-roh-DACK-till-us) was the first-ever pterosaur to be discovered.

DID RHAMPHORHYNCHUS HAVE FEATHERED WINGS?

Like all pterosaurs, Rhamphorhynchus (RAM-for-ink-us) did not have feathered wings for flying. Instead, it had leathery wings covered with skin, like those of a bat. Attached to the wings were clawed fingers used to catch and grip prey. Light, hollow bones helped Rhamphorhynchus stay airborne.

WAS QUETZALCOATLUS THE LARGEST FLIER?

With a wingspan of 12 m (39 ft), Quetzalcoatlus (KWETS-ul-koh-AT-lus) is believed to be one of the largest fliers of all time. No one is sure whether Quetzalcoatlus hunted mostly at sea or on land, but studies have shown that it could have flown for long distances looking for food. Its top speed in the air is believed to be 128 km/h (80 mph).

WHY DID ELASMOSAURUS HAVE A LONG NECK?

Elasmosaurus (el-LAZZ-moh-SORE-us) belonged to a group of marine reptiles known as plesiosaurs, which often had long necks, similar to sauropod dinosaurs on land. It is thought that Elasmosaurus used its long neck to grab hard-to-reach prey and flick them quickly into its mouth.

WHICH REPTILES CONTROLLED THE SEAS?

While dinosaurs were the reptiles that lived on land, and pterosaurs were the reptiles that ruled the air, a different group of giant reptiles dominated the seas. These massive marine reptiles were equipped with sleek, streamlined bodies to help them swim easily through the water and seek out their prey. Dakosaurus (DACK-oh-sore-us) was a marine predator around the size of a large crocodile that lived during the Early Cretaceous period.

DID YOU KNOW?

Kronosaurus (KRON-o-sore-us) was one of the largest and most lethal creatures to live in the sea, and it would have dwarfed a modern-day shark. Belonging to the pliosaur group of marine reptiles, Kronosaurus could reach up to 10 m (33 ft) long and weigh 1,000 kg (2,204 lb). It had a short neck, broad flippers, and a long jaw. It used its powerful bite to grip and then crush its prey.

WERE MANY OF THE DINOSAURS PLANT-EATERS?

Most of the dinosaurs were herbivores, which means that they ate plants. Some herbivores, such as Triceratops (try-SEH-ra-tops), were low to the ground and had horns and beaks. Others, such as Hadrosaurus (HAD-roh-sore-us), had less protection but developed special teeth to chew their food. The herbivores known as sauropods grew to sizes never seen before or after on Earth.

WHAT DOES "THEROPOD" MEAN?

All of the meat-eating dinosaurs belonged to the theropod group, which means "beast-footed." Large theropods were perfectly designed killing machines with a big head, thick neck, and powerful legs. These predators would use their feet to hold down their prey and tear off chunks. Smaller theropods, such as Struthiomimus (stroo-thee-OH-meem-us), were quick and agile and used their long claws to hunt.

DID ALL MEAT-EATERS HAVE SHARP TEETH?

Not all two-legged dinosaurs had sharp teeth. Gallimimus (gal-ee-MY-mus) was about the size of a turkey and had a beak instead of a snout. It used this beak to eat aquatic insects and crush up seeds.

HOW DID DINOSAURS REPRODUCE?

Dinosaurs gave birth by laying eggs, as reptiles and birds do today. Some dinosaurs, such as Oviraptor (OH-vee-rap-tor), sat on their eggs to warm them. Others, such as Argentinosaurus (AR-jen-tee-noh-sore-us), laid thousands of eggs in colonies and left them to hatch by themselves.

DID DINOSAURS EAT EGGS?

Meat-eaters would have found eggs and young hatchlings an easy meal. Some dinosaurs guarded their nests. Protoceratops (proh-toh-SERRA-tops) laid their eggs in a circle of hollowed-out ground with a wall of earth to protect them. They stayed close to the nest to protect it from predators.

DID DINOSAURS SIT ON THEIR NESTS LIKE BIRDS?

Oviraptor guarded its own nest—a hollow dug in the ground. We know that it sat on its eggs until they hatched.

WHAT WAS A DINOSAUR EGG LIKE?

Dinosaur eggs had a hard outer casing, like birds' eggs, and came in several shapes and sizes. Most were elongated, but the eggs of Diplodocus were the size and shape of a soccer ball. Maiasaura's (MY-ah-sore-ah's) eggs, shown here, were oval-shaped and were the size of a grapefruit.

DID DINOSAURS LIVE IN HERDS?

For many plant-eating dinosaurs, living in a herd provided safety in numbers. Giant sauropods, such as Saltasaurus (SOL-tuh-sore-us), kept their babies in the middle of the herd where they could be protected. Large adults stayed on the outside of the herd to watch out for predators.

DID DINOSAURS MIGRATE?

Large sauropods are likely to have migrated during the summer months, much like herds of zebra do today. By looking at fossils of sauropod teeth and analyzing what they ate, scientists can track the dinosaurs' movements. It is thought that they moved from the plains to upland areas in search of food each summer. Dinosaur trackways have been found all over the world, from Canada in the north to Australia in the south.

HOW DID DINOSAURS COMMUNICATE?

Plant-eating dinosaurs warned each other of danger by flushing their body parts with blood, flapping their feathers, or making loud noises. Some developed special ways of making themselves heard. Parasaurolophus (pa-ra-sore-OLL-off-us) used the crest on top of its head to make honking and hooting sounds. A recent theory suggested that the warning noises a Parasaurolophus made sounded like a foghorn on a boat.

WHO WERE THE LARGEST DINOSAURS?

The largest dinosaurs were the plant-eating sauropods. The sauropods had bulky bodies, tiny heads, tall legs, and incredibly long tails and necks. The design of a sauropod is much like that of a crane on a building site. Its bulky body kept it from toppling over.

HOW THICK WAS DINOSAUR SKIN?

Dinosaur skin was tough and scaly like that of modern reptiles. The skin had to be strong enough to not tear easily but flexible for freedom of movement. It also had to be waterproof to protect against the elements. Waterproof skin prevents an animal from drying out in the sun as well as keeping liquid from getting in.

WHAT SHADES WERE DINOSAURS?

The giant sauropods are thought to have been drab shades, such as green and brown. The meat-eaters were probably striped and spotted like a leopard or tiger to help camouflage them when they were hunting.

WAS BRACHIOSAURUS THE BIGGEST DINOSAUR?

When the bones of Brachiosaurus (BRAK-ee-oh-SORE-us) were discovered in 1903, scientists believed it to be the biggest creature that ever walked the planet. Brachiosaurus was longer than three buses and heavier than nine elephants. But despite its enormous size, Brachiosaurus was dwarfed by an even bigger dinosaur discovered in 1993: Argentinosaurus.

WHAT WAS THE BIGGEST SAUROPOD OF ALL?

As long as four buses and weighing more than 12 elephants, Argentinosaurus was the biggest sauropod of all. It lived in South America during the Late Cretaceous period.

HOW TALL WAS A BRACHIOSAURUS LEG?

Brachiosaurus was unusual for a sauropod dinosaur because its front legs were longer than its back legs. Its front legs were taller than a human and kept the head of the dinosaur raised upward. This helped the dinosaur reach the highest leaves at the tops of tall trees.

HOW DID DIPLODOCUS EAT?

Diplodocus had distinctive pencil-shaped teeth that were arranged like a rake at the front of its jaws. There were no back teeth to chew, so Diplodocus spent its time raking leaves off the trees and swallowing them. Although it could reach the treetops, it is thought that Diplodocus kept its head horizontal most of the time, sweeping its head backward and forward like a vacuum cleaner over the trees.

WHY DID PLANT-EATERS HAVE LONG NECKS?

The giant sauropod dinosaurs had long necks to reach the high leaves that other plant-eaters could not reach. Because they were so large, sauropods had to eat a tremendous amount of leaves each day to survive. By being able to reach the highest leaves, the sauropods were not competing with other, smaller herbivores for their food.

DID YOU KNOW?

Diplodocus was 29 m (95 ft) long, 4 m (13 ft) high, and weighed 14,500 kg (32,000 lb).

COULD DIPLODOCUS STAND ON ITS BACK LEGS?

Diplodocus was one of the longest dinosaurs. Its enormous tail may have been used to balance its very long neck. Diplodocus may have made itself even taller by standing on its back legs to reach the highest branches. If it did so, its tail would have rested on the ground and helped prevent it from toppling over.

HOW DID THE GIANT PLANT-EATERS GET SO BIG?

The sauropods became so big by making themselves the ultimate eating machines. They did this by developing their bodies to consume the greatest number of calories as quickly as possible. This was made possible by the blossoming of new plant and forest life that took place during the Jurassic period.

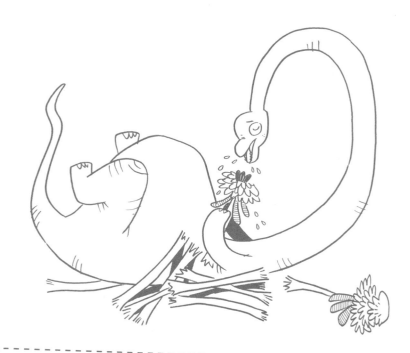

HOW DID THE SAUROPODS DIGEST THEIR FOOD?

Because the sauropods ate so much, they did not have time to chew their food. Instead, they swallowed it whole and left their stomach to do the rest. To help with this task, sauropods swallowed stones called gastroliths, which helped grind up their food. When a gastrolith became too smooth, the sauropod expelled it and swallowed a new one. Piles of smooth gastrolith stones have been found among dinosaur fossils in the Morrison Formation, a large series of rock layers in North America.

HOW MUCH DID THE SAUROPODS EAT?

A large sauropod like Diplodocus had to eat around 520 kg (1,150 lb) of plant material every day just to survive. Argentinosaurus probably had to eat even more. As it grew from a 5 kg (11 lb) hatchling, Argentinosaurus gained up to 40 kg (90 lb) of weight every day. It took around 40 years for Argentinosaurus to reach its maximum weight of 75,000 kg (165,350 lb).

WAS T. REX RELATED TO GIGANOTOSAURUS?

Giganotosaurus (gig-an-OH-toe-sore-us) roamed the Earth 30 million years before T. rex existed, and the two were not directly related. Instead, Giganotosaurus was related to another huge killer named Carcharodontosaurus (kar-KAR-oh-don-toh-sore-us). However, Carcharodontosaurus lived in Africa, and there was no chance of it battling Giganotosaurus for dominance.

DID THE GIANT PLANT-EATERS HAVE ENEMIES?

For every large plant-eater that walked the Earth, there was also a large meat-eater to rival it. On the plains of South America, Argentinosaurus evolved into the biggest dinosaur the world has ever known. However, at the same time, a great meat-eater grew alongside it: Giganotosaurus. It is unlikely that a Giganotosaurus would have tried to bring down an Argentinosaurus by itself, but it probably hunted in packs to do so.

HOW BIG WAS GIGANOTOSAURUS?

Giganotosaurus was the largest meat-eating dinosaur of South America in the Cretaceous period, and a terror to any plant-eater that crossed its path. Giganotosaurus weighed more than two elephants, was as long as two buses, and had jaws full of long, serrated teeth, ideal for slicing through bone and flesh.

WHO WAS THE BIGGEST PLATED DINOSAUR?

Ankylosaurus (ankle-OH-sore-us) was the tank of the dinosaur world. The largest member of the ankylosaur family, Ankylosaurus was armed with deadly weapons, covered in impenetrable plates, and weighed as much as a small bus. Ankylosaurus needed this level of protection; the plant-eater lived during the time of the terrifying tyrannosaurs.

HOW LONG WERE TRICERATOPS'S HORNS?

Triceratops, or "three-horned face," was named after its short nose horn and two long brow horns. The dinosaur's nose horn was only around 30 cm (12 in) long, but its sharp brow horns could reach 1 m (3 ft) each. These provided protection against predators such as T. rex.

WHY DID SOME DINOSAURS HAVE FRILLS?

There were several reasons why some dinosaurs had bright neck frills. These were used to signal to other dinosaurs, attract mates, scare off predators, and possibly collect heat from the sun. Triceratops' large, bony frill also protected its neck from dinosaur bites.

DID TRICERATOPS LIVE IN HERDS?

Experts think that Triceratops lived alone or in small family groups. However, many plant-eating dinosaurs did move in herds for protection against large meat-eaters. In a herd, dinosaurs could warn each other of danger and join together against predators.

WAS T. REX THE BIGGEST TYRANNOSAUR?

The most famous, feared, and ferocious dinosaur of all time, Tyrannosaurus rex was the great heavyweight of the Cretaceous period. T. rex's terrible reputation was well-founded: It was the biggest and most powerful of all of the tyrannosaur predators, and one of the most spectacular killers that has ever walked the planet.

DID T. REX HAVE FEATHERS?

In recent times, it has been suggested that T. rex had a layer of feathers around its head, although no one can be sure.

WHAT WERE T. REX'S TEETH LIKE?

T. rex's teeth were among the largest teeth of any land creature and could easily crunch through bone.

DID T. REX HAVE A BIG BRAIN?

T. rex had one of the largest and most developed brains of the predatory dinosaurs. The part of the brain responsible for smell was particularly acute. T. rex was also armed with forward-facing eyes, which gave it binocular vision and a greater ability to sense depth. These senses combined to give T. rex a formidable advantage over its prey.

WHAT WERE A KILLER DINOSAUR'S WEAPONS?

Every meat-eating dinosaur had a deadly array of weapons in its arsenal to hunt down and kill its prey. These weapons included teeth, claws, and jaws, but size, speed, and strength also helped. Most importantly, the predators needed bigger brains than their prey to outsmart them.

COULD THE DINOSAURS RUN?

Because dinosaurs could walk, it is likely that most would have been able to run. To work out a dinosaur's rough speed, paleontologists (scientists who study dinosaur fossils) measure the distance between fossilized dinosaur footprints and the size of the tracks. But they need to find a good set of prints to do this!

WHO WERE THE GREATEST KILLER DINOSAURS?

Enormous predatory dinosaurs were the terror of the Mesozoic Era. These fearsome killers stalked and hunted live prey, scavenged meat from dead carcasses, and even ate one another. The most famous and ferocious of the large predators included T. rex, Allosaurus (AL-oh-saw-rus), and Tarbosaurus (TAR-boh-sore-us).

WERE ALL "RAPTORS" ACTUALLY RAPTORS?

Some, but not all, dinosaurs with "raptor" in their name belong to the dromaeosaurid family of feathered dinosaurs. Their titles can be deceptive, though. Many dromaeosaurs don't have "raptor" in their name, such as Deinonychus (die-NON-i-kus), Hesperonychus (hess-per-ON-ee-kus), and Saurornitholestes (sore-OR-nith-oh-less-teez). Others, such as Oviraptor and Eoraptor, aren't dromaeosaurs (raptors) at all. True dromaeosaurs include Microraptor (MY-cro-rap-tor), Bambiraptor (bam-BEE-rap-tor), Dakotaraptor (dah-KO-tah-rap-tor), Utahraptor (U-tah-rap-tor), and the famous Velociraptor (vel-OSS-ee-rap-tor).

WHICH KILLER HAD LETHAL CLAWS?

An unusual predator named Megaraptor (MEG-a-rap-tor) had one of the most lethal claws ever discovered on a dinosaur. Megaraptor was an 8 m (26 ft) long monster with a sickle-shaped hand claw that measured 35 cm (14 in) long. That's longer than a fork! The claw was the longest of several claws that Megaraptor used to slash open its prey.

WHO DID DEINONYCHUS HUNT?

The most common of Deinonychus's prey was the plant-eating Tenontosaurus (ten-ON-toe-sore-us). We know this because a deposit of fossils found in North America revealed several Deinonychus skeletons around those of a Tenontosaurus. This fossil find also proved that the raptor hunted in packs.

WHY DID VELOCIRAPTOR HAVE FEATHERS?

Often dinosaurs had feathers to attract or alarm other dinosaurs, but it is thought that Velociraptor used them for insulation. Feathers would have kept Velociraptor warm as it went about its active, hunting lifestyle.

DID ALLOSAURUS AMBUSH ITS PREY?

Hundreds of Allosaurus fossils have been discovered in recent times, so we know a lot about this huge Late Jurassic killer. Allosaurus was the biggest predator of its time and certainly capable of hunting large prey. However, to obtain an advantage, Allosaurus would have lain in wait and then pounced on passing creatures.

DID ALLOSAURUS HUNT LARGE PREY?

Allosaurus bite marks found in the fossilized remains of Stegosaurus and some sauropods indicate that it brought down large prey. It may have hunted in packs to do so, as did its allosaur cousins, Sinraptor (SINE-rap-tor) and Yangchuanosaurus (yang-choo-AHN-oh-sore-us).

DID DASPLETOSAURUSES FIGHT ONE ANOTHER?

When the remains of a Daspletosaurus (das-PLEE-toh-sore-us) was discovered, it was obvious that the dinosaur was an ancestor to T. rex. Daspletosaurus resembled T. rex in almost every way, except that it was smaller, heavier, and had longer teeth. The bones also had bite marks made by another Daspletosaurus. This monster had been fighting its own kind.

DID ANY MEAT-EATING DINOSAURS ALSO EAT PLANTS?

Ornithomimus (or-nith-oh-MEE-mus) was a theropod that was unlike any other predatory dinosaur. Most theropods were either hunters that preyed on mammals and other little dinosaurs or large monsters that preyed on the large plant-eaters. But Ornithomimus was neither of these—it was a meat-eater that also ate plants.

DID YOU KNOW?

Daspletosaurus grew up to 9 m (30 ft) long and weighed up to 3,700 kg (8,200 lb).

HOW DID DASPLETOSAURUS HUNT?

Like a lion in a pride, Daspletosaurus was a pack hunter that would cooperate with other Daspletosauruses to bring down prey. However, Daspletosaurus was also an opportunist, and it is unlikely that these group kills were well organized. Instead, several Daspletosauruses would have grabbed their chance to join together and attack an isolated plant-eater.

HOW DO WE KNOW ORNITHOMIMUS ATE PLANTS?

We know that Ornithomimus ate plants as well as meat because it had a long beak instead of a mouth. This scissorlike beak would have been used to pick up insects and small reptiles, but also to strip and slice through leaves and other plant material.

WAS ORNITHOMIMUS A BIRD?

"Ornithomimus" means "bird mimic," and its feathers and size made it look a lot like a modern ostrich. But Ornithomimus was not a bird—it was a theropod that belonged to the ornithomimid group of dinosaurs. The ornithomimids all had feathers, slender arms and claws, long legs, and could achieve fast running speeds.

DID YOU KNOW?

Baryonyx grew to 10 m (32 ft) long, 2.5 m (8 ft) high, and up to 5,400 kg (11,900 lb) in weight.

DID DINOSAURS EAT FISH?

In 1983, an amateur fossil hunter made a startling discovery in Surrey, England. He unearthed a massive fossil of a 25 cm (10 in) thumb claw. But there was more to come: Beneath the claw was the skeleton of an unknown dinosaur that ate both fish and meat. It was named Baryonyx (bah-ree-ON-iks).

HOW DID WE KNOW BARYONYX ATE BOTH MEAT AND FISH?

Fossils have revealed both fish scales and the remains of an Iguanodon in Baryonyx's stomach. As the largest meat-eating dinosaur discovered in Europe, it seems that Baryonyx could choose what it ate, mixing its diet between land- and water-dwelling prey.

WERE THERE ANY TINY DINOSAUR KILLERS?

Around 75 million years ago, giant meat-eaters like Daspletosaurus and Gorgosaurus (gorg-O-sore-us) prowled the plains, while small, speedy predators like Troodon and Struthiomimus stalked their prey in the forests. Alongside them, however, was an even smaller hunter: Hesperonychus was a killer dinosaur the size of a house cat.

HOW DID BARYONYX CATCH FISH?

Baryonyx probably stalked fish from the water's edge or stood in shallow rivers to catch them. Its long, curved claws would have been perfect for holding onto slippery fish. It also poked its snout into the water and grabbed passing fish with its long, crocodile-like jaws.

DID YOU KNOW?

Hesperonychus walked on two legs, had razor-sharp hand claws, and a sickle-shaped claw on its toe.

WHO WAS HESPERONYCHUS?

Hesperonychus was a Late Cretaceous killer believed to be the smallest predatory dinosaur in North America. Weighing up to 2 kg (4 lb), reaching 50 cm (1.5 ft) high, and armed with a mouthful of bladelike teeth, Hesperonychus looked like a miniature version of its cousin, Velociraptor. But unlike Velociraptor, Hesperonychus probably lived in the trees.

WAS HESPERONYCHUS ABLE TO FLY?

Hesperonychus was covered with feathers, but it could not fly like a bird. Instead, it glided on its wings between the branches of trees as it looked for food. Hesperonychus was small enough to go unnoticed by many large dinosaurs but would have made a good meal for others, so it kept off the forest floor. Hesperonychus's own diet included lizards, insects, and eggs.

HOW DID PLANT-EATERS PROTECT THEMSELVES?

Size was a plant-eater's best defense against an attacking meat-eater. A massive sauropod like Argentinosaurus was too big to be threatened by a single predator. Other, smaller plant-eaters developed their own individual ways of protecting themselves. These included spikes, horns, and thick plates in their skin.

HOW DID GASTONIA USE ITS SPIKES?

Gastonia (gas-TOH-nee-ah) was a heavily protected ankylosaur. It grew to 4.6 m (15 ft) in length and weighed up to 3,360 kg (7,400 lb). The spikes along its back stopped enemies such as Utahraptor from leaping up and biting its neck. Gastonia was also able to fight back with its deadly spike-covered tail.

HOW DID CHASMOSAURUS USE ITS FRILL?

Chasmosaurus was a ceratopsian dinosaur and one of the most common to roam the plains of North America. It had a large head frill, but since it was made from thin bone and skin, it would have offered little protection. However, by flushing blood into the skin stretched across the frill, Chasmosaurus may have been able to warn off potential attackers.

DID YOU KNOW?
Stegosaurus lived during the Late Jurassic period, and fossils have been found on several continents.

DID STEGOSAURUS USE ITS TAIL TO FIGHT?

With the row of plates down its back and the spikes at the end of its tail, Stegosaurus is easy to recognize. The tail is called a thagomizer, and it was an essential weapon against the top predator of the period and Stegosaurus's archenemy: Allosaurus.

DID DINOSAURS FIGHT WITH THEIR HEADS?

For many plant-eating dinosaurs, their primary weapon was located on their head. These weapons included spikes and horns on the nose, face, and frill, such as those of the ceratopsian Styracosaurus. Another plant-eater named Pachycephalosaurus (pack-ee-KEF-ah-loh-sore-us) may have used its hard, bony head to butt against attackers.

HOW MANY HORNS DID STYRACOSAURUS HAVE?

Styracosaurus had up to nine head horns—more than any other ceratopsian! Small horns on its cheeks ran up to meet longer horns on Styracosaurus's frill. But Styracosaurus's nose horn was the longest of all, and at 30 cm (2 ft) long, it would have been deadly against predators such as Daspletosaurus.

WAS PACHYCEPHALOSAURUS A HEAD-BUTTER?

One of the strangest dinosaurs ever discovered, Pachycephalosaurus had a thick head dome made from 25 cm (10 in) of solid bone. This prompted the theory that Pachycephalosaurus used its dome to head-butt enemies and rival Pachycephalosauruses. A discovery in 2012 supported this theory. A Pachycephalosaurus skull was unearthed that showed damage that had probably resulted from head-butting.

WHO WAS CARCHARODONTOSAURUS?

During the Late Cretaceous period, Carcharodontosaurus was the largest land hunter in North Africa. Its head was larger than T. rex's, and it contained a mouthful of long, bladelike teeth like a shark's. Carcharodontosaurus needed to eat 60 kg (130 lb) of meat every day to survive, and each one defended a piece of territory around 500 sq km (200 sq mi).

DID MEAT-EATING DINOSAURS OFTEN FIGHT?

As a rule, different species of large, predatory dinosaurs tried to avoid each other. Each dominated its own patch, and unless food became scarce, it was not worth waging a territorial war. However, occasionally, such battles did take place. We know about one between Spinosaurus (SPY-noh-sore-us) and Carcharodontosaurus, two of the largest predators to walk the Earth.

DID YOU KNOW?

Carcharodontosaurus, or "shark-toothed lizard," was named after the great white shark (Carcharodon) because of the resemblance between their serrated teeth.

DID TRICERATOPS EVER FIGHT T. REX?

Triceratops and T. rex were the two mightiest dinosaurs to prowl the plains and forests of Late Cretaceous North America. The image of T. rex, its jaws bristling with bone-crunching teeth, battling the tank-shaped Triceratops, with its face full of horns, is spectacular and terrifying. But there is very little evidence of a T. rex and Triceratops battle.

DID ARGENTINOSAURUS HAVE A PREDATOR?

At first, it was thought unlikely that there was a predator big enough to hunt Argentinosaurus. But in 2006, a new discovery made experts think again. A new, 13 m (43 ft) long killer had been found, and it was capable of hunting a giant like Argentinosaurus. This dinosaur was named Mapusaurus (MAH-puh-sore-us).

DID YOU KNOW?

Fossils have shown T. rex's bite marks on Triceratops bones, but these are thought to have occurred after death. In other words, T. rex probably scavenged from a Triceratops carcass after it was already dead. More gruesomely, the injuries show that T. rex removed Triceratops's head to get at the nutrient-rich flesh in its neck.

DID YOU KNOW?

Mapusaurus was closely related to Giganotosaurus, which also roamed the plains of South America.

WERE DINOSAURS CANNIBALS?

During the Late Cretaceous period, two types of killer dinosaurs dominated the Earth. The northern hemisphere was ruled by the tyrannosaurs and the southern hemisphere, by the abelisaurs. Abelisaurs were just as dangerous and deadly as their northern counterparts and also had a disturbing habit: cannibalism.

WERE ANY DINOSAURS POISONOUS?

The discovery of Sinornithosaurus (sine-OR-nith-oh-sore-us) was a world-changing moment in the study of dinosaurs. The feathers covering this so-called "fuzzy raptor" were almost identical to that of modern birds. Sinornithosaurus was a true ancestor to the birds. But there was more: It also had specially shaped teeth that could inject poison into its prey.

WHO WAS MAJUNGASAURUS?

Majungasaurus (mah-JOONG-gah-sore-us) was a common abelisaur that left many fossils behind. The bones of these fossils have revealed a series of deep bite marks made by other Majungasauruses. These marks show that the dinosaurs not only fought each other, but that they also ate the flesh off each other's bones. It is the first direct evidence of cannibalism in dinosaurs.

COULD DIPLODOCUS WHIP ITS TAIL?

At the end of Diplodocus's tail were small, tube-shaped vertebrae that would have made a dangerous whip. Many sauropods used their tail as a whip to fend off predators, and it is likely that Diplodocus did the same. Diplodocus would have also used its tail to balance itself when it reared up on its hind feet.

WHY WERE DINOSAURS RECORD-BREAKERS?

By their very nature, dinosaurs were record-breakers. They dominated the globe for tens of millions of years and in that time were among the largest, longest, and most lethal creatures the world has ever known. But dinosaurs weren't only famous for their size and strength: Some were smart, others stupid, and some were the speediest creatures around.

WHAT WERE SINORNITHOSAURUS'S TEETH LIKE?

Sinornithosaurus had long, fang-like teeth with a groove running down the surface. This type of tooth is usually only seen in venomous animals, such as snakes. Experts think that a venom gland in the jaw fed poison into the teeth. When Sinornithosaurus bit into its victim with its fangs, the poison would then have stunned or killed its prey.

DID YOU KNOW?

Titanosaur fossils have been found on every continent. They are particularly common in Australia and South America.

DID ARGENTINOSAURUS LAY BIG EGGS?

Argentinosaurus eggs were about the size of footballs. More impressive is the number of eggs it laid. An enormous fossil bed in Argentina has revealed tens of thousands of Argentinosaurus eggs. It is thought that the area was used as a nesting site for the sauropods over millions of years, with each one laying hundreds of eggs annually.

WHICH DINOSAUR WAS THE BIGGEST?

The biggest dinosaur was also the largest creature ever to walk on land: Argentinosaurus. Argentinosaurus lived during the Early Cretaceous period in South America. It was half the length of a 747 passenger plane, weighed the same as 1,000 grown men, and was tall enough to have peered through the windows of a building four floors high.

WHICH WAS THE BIGGEST DINOSAUR PREDATOR?

The largest land carnivore ever seen on Earth was Spinosaurus. Spinosaurus roamed the swamps of North Africa during the Cretaceous Period. It was a colossal killer with a list of massive measurements. It was longer than two buses, taller than a giraffe, and weighed more than 30 lions. Its skull measured 2 m (6.5 ft)—that's the longest of any theropod dinosaur.

WHICH DINOSAUR WAS THE SMARTEST?

The smartest dinosaur is thought to be Troodon. That is because this meat-eater had the biggest brain in relation to its body size of any dinosaur. Even so, it was no Einstein; it is thought that Troodon had a similar level of intelligence to modern-day birds.

DID YOU KNOW?

Troodon's brain was about the size of a modern emu's. Emus also have large eyes for their size, giving them good eyesight.

$$Gui=891\ G(Tw+tP)$$

COULD TROODON HUNT AT NIGHT?

Troodon had extremely big eyes, which allowed it to see more in low-light conditions. The Troodons of Alaska used this well-adapted eyesight to hunt at night, something that was not possible for most other predators. Troodons often targeted young Edmontosaurus (ed-MON-toe-sore-us) under the cover of night. The Alaskan Troodons were so successful in this that they grew to twice the size of Troodons anywhere else in the world.

HOW BIG WAS TROODON?

Troodon was about the size of a large dog. It was also fast. Troodon had long, thin legs and a large toe claw, which it could retract like a cat's when it was running. It was also a pack hunter and made good use of its speed and high intelligence to outsmart its prey.

WHICH DINOSAUR WAS THE WEIRDEST?

There were lots of odd dinosaurs, from the head-butting Pachycephalosaurus to the ill-equipped Iguanodon, which had only a thumb spike for protection. But perhaps the strangest of all was Therizinosaurus (THER-ih-zine-oh-sore-us). Therizinosaurus was a large theropod with a twist: It had given up eating meat to become a vegetarian.

DID YOU KNOW?

The dromaeosaur dinosaurs, such as Troodon, had the biggest brains for their body size.

WHICH DINOSAUR HAD THE SMALLEST BRAIN?

With its distinctive back plates and spiked tail, Stegosaurus is one of the most famous plant-eating dinosaurs. It was also one of the stupidest. Although it weighed more than a rhinoceros, Stegosaurus had the brain the size of a walnut. This is especially surprising because Stegosaurus's head was the same size as the head of a horse.

WHICH DINOSAURS WERE THE FASTEST?

The small- to medium-sized theropods were the fastest runners of the dinosaur world. However, calculating any dinosaur's running speed can be a tricky task. To do this, the dinosaur's footprints left in trackways have to be measured against its fossilized leg bones. This gives a speed estimate.

WHICH WERE THE SMALLEST DINOSAURS?

A large number of small dinosaurs came and went during the Mesozoic Era. Every time scientists think they have discovered the smallest-ever dinosaur, another, even tinier one is found to take its place.

MICRORAPTOR

This was a crow-sized killer around 80 cm long (31 in) long and 2 kg (4.4 lb) in weight. It lived in China during the Early Cretaceous period.

ANCHIORNIS

A kitten-sized, feathered dinosaur, Anchiornis (ang-KEE-or-nis) grew up to 34 cm (13 in) long. It lived in China during the Jurassic Period and, at only 110 g (3.9 oz), is the lightest dinosaur ever discovered.

HESPERONYCHUS

This was a pigeon-sized Late Cretaceous predator from North America that grew up to 50 cm (1.5 ft) long and 2 kg (4 lb) in weight.

COMPSOGNATHUS

A chicken-sized theropod, Compsognathus (komp-sog-NATH-us) was around 65 cm (26 in) long and 3.6 kg (8 lb) in weight. It stalked its prey in Europe during the Late Jurassic period.

WHICH DINOSAUR HAD THE BIGGEST HEAD?

The dinosaurs with the largest heads were the horned and frilled herbivores known as the ceratopsians. The heads of these giants were so big that they sometimes made up 40 percent of their overall body length. The award for biggest-ever head goes jointly to two ceratopsian cousins: Torosaurus (tor-OH-sore-us) and Pentaceratops (pen-tah-SERRA-tops).

WERE FRILLS USED FOR PROTECTION?

The frills of Pentaceratops and Torosaurus were made from thin bone with two large openings in the middle, so they would not have been used for protection.

HOW BIG WAS TOROSAURUS'S HEAD?

Torosaurus was closely related to Triceratops and had a similar frill and horns. The length of Torosaurus's head, which includes its frill, was 2.77 m (9.1 ft). That's as long as a small car! Torosaurus's skull is thought to be the longest of any known land animal that has lived on Earth.

WHICH WAS THE BIGGEST FEATHERED DINOSAUR?

The bones of the largest feathered dinosaur were found by accident in 2005. Paleontologists were making a film in China about sauropod bones when they discovered a mysterious bone buried among them. It was the leg bone of Gigantoraptor (gig-ANT-oh-rap-tor): the biggest feathered creature that ever walked the Earth. It was similar in appearance to another strange theropod: Therizinosaurus.

HOW BIG WAS GIGANTORAPTOR?

At over 2,200 kg (4,850 lb), Gigantoraptor weighed more than 14 ostriches, which is the heaviest feathered creature alive today. Gigantoraptor was also 8 m (26 ft) long, which is 35 times larger than its nearest oviraptor cousin and not much smaller than T. rex. Like other oviraptors, Gigantoraptor was armed with large killing claws on its feet and could easily outrun most theropod predators. Gigantoraptor had wings but flapped them only in display. It also laid some of the biggest dinosaur eggs ever discovered.

DID YOU KNOW?

The first vertebrates to develop true flight were the pterosaurs, but they later shared the skies with Microraptor and early birds.

DID YOU KNOW?

Gigantoraptor had a beak for a mouth, and it is thought that it ate plants, insects, and small mammals, but no one is sure.

DID YOU KNOW?

A cure for whooping cough used in Yorkshire, England, in the 1800s was to drink a bowl of soup with nine frogs hidden in it. You couldn't make it yourself—it only worked if you didn't know about the frogs. (And probably not then, either!)

HOW WERE HEADACHES CURED IN THE STONE AGE?

Many tribes around the world have performed trepanning since the Stone Age. It involves drilling a hole in the skull, often with a stone, to ease headaches by letting out evil spirits. People frequently survived, because many skulls have been found with several such holes, some partially healed.

WHAT IS MALARIA?

Malaria is a deadly disease spread by mosquitoes. It's caused by a tiny parasite that lives inside a person's blood cells. Malaria kills up to three million people a year.

HOW WERE ANTS USED IN SURGERY?

Early Indian surgeons used ants to hold the edges of wounds together. They would get an ant to bite through both sides of the wound, then twist off the ant's body and throw it away, leaving the head in place with the jaws acting as a stitch.

HOW DID GOLDFISH SAVE LIVES IN WWI?

During World War I, goldfish were used to check whether all traces of poisonous gas had been washed out of gas masks. The mask was rinsed and filled with water, then a goldfish was dropped in. If it died, there was still gas left in it.

HOW DID A BULLET WOUND HELP A DOCTOR'S STUDIES?

In 1822, Dr. William Beaumont studied human digestion as it happened, through a hole in the side and stomach of a patient who had been shot. The hole didn't heal, allowing Dr. Beaumont to study, but also allowing food and drink to ooze out if it wasn't covered up.

DID YOU KNOW?

In an attempt to kill malaria-carrying mosquitoes, an American scientist built towers to attract bats. He enticed them in with fabric covered with bat droppings and played music near the bats' old homes to drive them out. After a few years, malaria infection dropped from 89 percent of the population to zero.

DID YOU KNOW?

Horses killed in World War I were recycled as explosives—their fat was removed and boiled down to be used in making TNT.

HOW DO RATS FIND LANDMINES?

Rats trained to look for landmines are so light that they don't trigger the mechanism if they step on one. Instead, they scratch and bite at the ground when they smell explosives, and the handler deals with the mine.

HOW CAN MAGGOTS HELP SURGEONS?

One of the best ways of cleaning an infected wound is to put maggots into it to eat the rotting flesh. This was used before the days of antibiotics and now with infections that antibiotics can't treat.

DID YOU KNOW?

Taking a bath in the water used to wash a corpse was thought to cure epilepsy.

WHEN IS HONEY DEADLY?

A toxin in the nectar of laurels and rhododendrons causes honey made from these plants to be poisonous. In 66 BCE, Roman troops were lured by their enemies into a grove where bees made honey from these flowers. The soldiers ate it and were slaughtered while sick.

CAN POTATOES KILL YOU?

Green potatoes contain a poison, solanine, which can be deadly. It develops in old potatoes that aren't kept in the dark. Eating 2 kg (4.4 lb) of green potatoes could be fatal.

HOW CAN FIREFLIES HELP SCIENTISTS?

Scientists investigating abnormal lumps added a gene from a firefly to make a glow-in-the-dark lump. The lump is visible through the skin of a test animal, so scientists can see if it grows or shrinks.

HOW CAN YOU TELL THE AGE OF A DEAD BODY?

Police scientists investigating a murder can tell how long a body has been dead by looking at the kinds of maggots, worms, and insects that are eating it.

COULD BLUE WHALES LIVE ON LAND?

If blue whales tried to live on land, they would be crushed and suffocated by their own weight. They can live successfully in water because it supports them.

WHICH ANIMALS WERE USED TO DETECT GAS?

Some animals respond to small amounts of poisonous gas and have been used as early warning systems. German soldiers kept cats in the trenches of World War I to smell gas, and British miners kept budgerigars in cages because they died quickly if gas escaped into the mine.

HOW LONG DOES IT TAKE A DEAD WHALE TO DISAPPEAR?

It can take 100 years for the body of a whale at the bottom of the sea to disappear completely as it is slowly eaten away by different animals, plants, and microbes.

CAN A MOUSE SURVIVE A FALL FROM A GREAT HEIGHT?

A small animal such as a mouse can be dropped 1,000 m (3,280 ft) down a mine shaft and suffer no harm, because the fastest speed it can fall is not enough to crush its body. The larger an animal or object, the shorter the distance it can safely fall.

DID YOU KNOW?

Scraping rotten parts off your food doesn't get rid of them—behind the fuzzy parts you can see, strings extend into the food up to nine times the length of the visible areas.

WHOSE POOP WAS AS PRICEY AS GOLD?

Italian artist Piero Manzoni filled 90 small cans with his own poop for a 1961 exhibition. They were sold to art buyers at a price equal to their weight in gold!

HOW MUCH EARTH DO WORMS MOVE?

Earthworms bring 4 million kg (8.8 million lb) of earth to the surface on every 1 sq km (0.38 sq mi) of open ground each year.

WHAT WAS THE ANCESTOR OF ALL VERTEBRATES?

Scientists believe that all vertebrates (animals with backbones) evolved from giant tadpoles, 6 cm (2.5 in) long, that swam around 550 million years ago.

DID YOU KNOW?

British hypnotist Bernadine Coady hypnotized herself so that she could have an operation on her knee without any medical pain relief.

WHAT'S THE BIGGEST LIVING THING IN THE WORLD?

The largest living thing in the world is a fungus in Washington State, which covers 6.5 sq km (2.5 sq mi) and has been growing for hundreds of years.

WHY SHOULD YOU FEAR A WILL-O'-THE-WISP?

A will-o'-the-wisp is a flame of burning marsh gas that appears in boggy areas at night. It has lured many wanderers to a muddy death when they left the path to follow it, believing it to be someone with a light.

WHY ARE SOME DEAD BODIES FROZEN?

Some wealthy people have their bodies cryopreserved (deep-frozen) when they die in the hope that in the future, someone will find a cure for their cause of death and resurrect them. The popular urban legend that Walt Disney was cryopreserved is false: He was cremated.

DID YOU KNOW?

In the USA, more than 150 pairs of identical twins are married to identical twins.

DID YOU KNOW?

Nearly one-fifth of the Earth's surface is dry desert where less than 25 cm (10 in) of rain falls in a year.

WHAT'S THE DEADLIEST NATURAL POISON?

The castor bean plant contains the most deadly poison in the natural world, ricin. Just 70 micrograms (two-millionths of an ounce) could kill an adult human. It's 12,000 times more poisonous than rattlesnake venom!

WHY DID SURGEONS BUY DEAD BODIES?

For centuries, it was illegal to cut up dead bodies, so surgeons and scientists had to pay criminals to steal the corpses of executed prisoners from the gallows in order to learn about anatomy.

WHAT'S THE SMELLIEST PLANT?

The stinking corpse plant, or Rafflesia, is a huge parasitic flower that smells like rotting meat. The flower is about 1 m (3 ft) across and is the largest flower in the world. It grows directly out of a creeping vine, from which it gains all its nourishment without ever growing leaves of its own.

DID YOU KNOW?

Lined up neatly, 10,000 bacteria would stretch across your thumbnail.

HOW FAST DOES BACTERIA REPRODUCE?

Bacteria—tiny living things that we also call germs—divide in two every 20 minutes. So, starting with one (it doesn't need a girlfriend/boyfriend), you can have over 130 million in just nine hours!

HOW CAN MUSEUMS USE BEETLES?

Dermestid beetles are so good at stripping the flesh off dead animals that natural history museums use their larvae to clean up skeletons they are going to put on display.

DID YOU KNOW?

The beetle with the longest body in the world is the the titan beetle (Titanus giganteus). It can measure up to 16.7 cm (6.6 in) in length.

HOW DO SCABS FORM?

Scabs are formed when chemical proteins react with special blood cells called platelets, which cause the cells to get sticky and clump together. Once they've clotted, lots of different chemicals and cells work together to dry out the clot and form a scab, keeping out germs while the cells underneath repair themselves. So if you pick a scab, you're tampering with all your body's hard work!

WHO INVENTED THE FROZEN CHICKEN?

The first frozen chicken was created by Sir Francis Bacon, who stuffed a plucked chicken with snow in 1626 to experiment with refrigeration. It worked, but Bacon died from a chill contracted during the experiment. The chicken is said to haunt Pond Square in London, England.

HOW DID FACE PAINT CAUSE DEATH?

In the past, people used white lead powder to make their skin look white, but it gave them lead poisoning and slowly killed them. Since their skin looked worse once the poison took effect, they used more white lead to cover up the damage.

WHAT'S THE MOST POISONOUS METAL?

The most poisonous metal in the world is arsenic. It used to be made into flypaper for killing flies, but it killed some people, too.

DID YOU KNOW?

In 2000, UK mountaineer Major Michael Lane gave a museum five of his own fingers and eight of his toes, which had dropped off as a result of frostbite when he was climbing Mount Everest in 1976.

WHY DID ENGINEERS BUILD A ROBOT KANGAROO?

There are over 20,000 road crashes involving kangaroos in Australia every year, so a robotic, kangaroo-like crash test dummy named Robo-Roo is used to test how badly cars will be damaged.

CAN YOU DROWN IN MUD?

It's possible to drown in mud—but really unlikely. If someone was drowning in mud, it would be almost impossible to save them since so much force is needed to pull them against the weight of it.

HOW DO DEODORANTS WORK?

Deodorants don't stop you from sweating, but they kill the bacteria that make sweat smell.

DID YOU KNOW?

Diamonds are so hard, they are often used as the tip of a dentist's drill because they can grind through teeth.

WHY DESIGN A ROBOT TADPOLE?

Scientists are working on a microscopic robotic tadpole to deliver medicines—the tadpole will "swim" through the patient's blood vessels to take the medicine where it's needed.

HOW BIG ARE BACTERIA?

Most bacteria are only 0.00025 of a centimeter (0.0001 of an inch) across. But monster bacteria have been found at the bottom of the ocean off the coast of Africa. They are so big, they can be seen without a microscope—they're each about the size of a pencil dot.

WHAT WOULD HAPPEN IF YOU FELL INTO A BLACK HOLE?

If you fell into a black hole, you would be stretched into an incredibly long, thin string in a process named "spaghettification."

WHAT IS IT LIKE TO PEE IN SPACE?

It is so cold in space that pee flushed out of a spacecraft instantly freezes into a stream of yellow crystals.

WHAT WILL WE DO WHEN WE RUN OUT OF OIL?

Among fuels investigated for use where (or when) oil and gas are scarce, scientists have tried running cars and tractors on chicken poop.

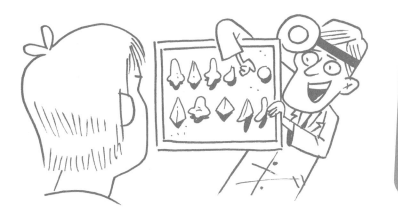

WHAT WAS THE FIRST COSMETIC SURGERY?

The earliest cosmetic surgery was done by doctors in India, who made fake noses for criminals whose noses had been cut off as a punishment for their crimes.

DID YOU KNOW?

In the 1600s and later, Egyptian mummies were ground up for use in medicines around Europe.

WHY SHOULD YOU NEVER TRY ANCIENT EGYPTIAN MEDICINE?

An ancient Egyptian who was feeling a bit unwell might eat a mixture of mashed mouse and poop. Yum! Bound to make you feel better!

HOW DID TOADS SELL MEDICINE?

Toadeaters were people employed by men selling medicine at fairs and markets. The toadeater had to swallow a toad—supposed to be deadly poisonous—and then take the medicine. Their survival encouraged people to buy the medicine. They may or may not have actually swallowed the toads ...

DOES IT EVER RAIN CATS AND DOGS?

No, but there have been rainstorms with falling fish, frogs, and toads! And once, in 1894, a turtle that was frozen inside a giant hailstone fell to Earth.

HOW OFTEN DO MAJOR DISASTERS HAPPEN?

In the last 550 million years, there have been five events that have each destroyed at least 50 percent of all life on the planet.

CAN IT RAIN BLOOD?

Old tales of a downpour of blood can be explained by red sand being picked up, carried vast distances in clouds, and falling with the rain.

DID YOU KNOW?

A lightning bolt is five times hotter than the surface of the sun.

HOW LARGE CAN HAILSTONES BE?

In 1849, a 6 m (20 ft) block of ice fell from the sky in Scotland as a giant hailstone! In one terrible storm in Bangladesh, 92 people were killed by hailstones that weighed over 1 kg (2.2 lb) each.

CAN WEATHER MAKE YOU GLOW?

In 1976, children playing in a school football game found that their heads began to glow. It was an appearance of St. Elmo's fire—a glow caused by the buildup of static electricity before a thunderstorm.

WHAT IS BALL LIGHTNING?

Ball lightning is the name given to fiery balls of electricity that whiz through the air, lasting several seconds. No one knows what causes them, and some scientists doubt they exist, even though there have been many sightings. In 1994, ball lightning left a hole in a closed window that measured 5 cm (2 in)!

HOW TALL ARE CLOUDS?

Some clouds are up to 20,000 m (65,616 ft) thick from top to bottom—more than three times as tall as Mount Everest.

WHERE IS THE WINDIEST PLACE ON EARTH?

Commonwealth Bay in Antarctica has the strongest winds of anywhere in the world—they blow at up to 322 km/h (200 mph).

WHERE IS THE RAINIEST PLACE ON EARTH?

Meghalaya in India has 1,187 mm (467 in) of rain a year, making it the rainiest place in the world.

HOW MUCH WATER IS IN THE CLOUDS?

Only 0.001 percent of the Earth's water is in clouds or falling rain at any one time.

DID YOU KNOW?

The word "hurricane" comes from the name Huracán, a Mayan god responsible for storms.

CAN TREES TALK TO EACH OTHER?

Some trees communicate using chemicals. If a wood-eating bug attacks one, the tree releases chemicals into the air, which prompt other trees in the area to produce a poison that deters the bugs.

CAN TREES WALK?

The walking or stilt palm walks to a better spot if it doesn't like where it's living! The tree grows up to 20 m (66 ft) tall in the Amazon. Stilts hold it up and support its central trunk. To move, the tree grows more stilts on one side, and then lets the other ones die so that it slowly moves along.

WHERE CAN YOU FIND THE TINIEST TREE?

The smallest type of tree is a dwarf willow that grows in Greenland. It is only 5 cm (2 in) tall.

DID YOU KNOW?

The Australian bloodwood tree oozes red sap that looks like blood when it is cut.

HOW LONG CAN TREES LIVE?

Some trees can live for a very long time. A redwood tree that fell over in California, USA, in 1977 is thought to have been 6,200 years old—which means it started to grow about 3,000 years before the reign of the first Ancient Egyptian king.

DO TREES EMPLOY GUARDS?

Instead of guard dogs, trumpet trees have "guard ants" living in their hollow limbs! In return for their home, the Azteca ants bite anything that nibbles on the tree and then squirt acid into the creature's wound to make it extra sore.

DID YOU KNOW?

There are 1,500 types of insects in a single rain forest tree in the Amazon, including 50 types of ants!

CAN YOU MIX A PLANT WITH AN ANIMAL?

Genetic engineering can combine genes from different plants and animals. A gene from a deep-sea fish can be added to a vegetable to make it frost resistant! Some people call these genetically modified foods "Frankenstein foods."

CAN YOU GROW A BRAZIL NUT TREE IN YOUR GARDEN?

Brazil nut trees grow happily in the rain forest environment but refuse to grow anywhere else in the world. Scientists have tried to remove them to cultivate in labs, but the trees don't like it.

WHAT IS THE DOOMSDAY VAULT?

A "doomsday vault" has been built in an Arctic cave to store seeds from all the world's food-giving plants in case a major disaster wipes them all out. It contains more than 860,000 seed samples that should be able to survive for up to 1,000 years.

IS THERE A PLANT THAT LOOKS LIKE POOP?

The Anacampseros albissima plant looks like a bird dropping to protect it from being eaten by animals.

DID YOU KNOW?

The pink petticoat plant has a flower that looks like a pretty petticoat—it might look nice, but it gobbles up bugs that crawl inside it.

WHAT PLANT EATS FLIES?

A Venus flytrap is a carnivorous plant that traps and eats flies. It doesn't strike quickly—it takes half an hour to squash a fly and kill it, and another 10 days to digest it.

DO PLANTS GROW IN DEAD BODIES?

Plants often grow inside the skeletons of dead bodies in the Arctic—they make warm homes and have lots of nutrients that nourish plants.

WHAT IS THE FASTEST-GROWING ORGANISM ON EARTH?

Some types of bamboo grow up to 91 cm (36 in) a day. This means that they are growing at a rate of 0.00003 km/h (0.00002 mph)! Meanwhile, the veiled lady mushroom grows faster than any other organism in the world. It grows up to 20 cm (8 in) in only 20 minutes, and it can be heard cracking as it grows!

HOW ABOUT A SLOW GROWER?

A cactus that grows in the Arizona desert grows less than 2.5 cm (1 in) in the first 10 years of its life. It's a slow starter!

WHAT PLANTS LOVE TO LIVE ON CORPSES?

Stinging nettles grow well in soil that contains dead bodies—they thrive on a chemical called phosphorous that can be found in the bones.

DID YOU KNOW?

A peanut is not really a nut—it grows underground!

DID YOU KNOW?

The South Pole has no sun for 182 days each year.

WHAT IS OIL MADE FROM?

Oil is made from the decayed bodies of animals and plants that died millions of years ago and have been squashed deep underground.

WHAT FLOWER SMELLS LIKE DEAD BODIES?

Several plants smell like dead bodies, including one called Amorphophallus titanum. Its stench is disgusting—it smells like a rotting corpse. This attracts insects that feed on the dead matter, and they pollinate the flower.

DID YOU KNOW?

The saguaro cactus can live for up to 200 years and grow to 18 m (59 ft) tall. It stores up to about 8 metric tonnes (8.8 tons) of water inside it—but don't cut one open for a drink in the desert, since it's poisonous to humans!

WHAT IS THE LARGEST LIVING THING ON EARTH?

In Oregon, USA, is a giant fungus that covers 10 sq km (3.86 sq mi) underground. It is thought to be around 2,400 years old but may even be up to 8,650 years old.

DID YOU KNOW?

The oceans provide 99 percent of the habitable space on Earth because they are so deep—on land, all plant and animal life is clustered on the surface.

CAN YOU FIND SEA CREATURES INLAND?

Lake Titicaca, on the border between Bolivia and Peru, is home to lots of sea creatures—but it's an inland lake. The lake was stranded when the landscape changed, trapping sea creatures in its saltwater environment.

DOES IT SNOW UNDERWATER?

The main source of food for animals that live in the deep sea is marine snow—flakes of dead things and poop from creatures who live higher up in the water!

WHAT IS A WATER DEVIL?

Water devils are small whirlwinds that make thin columns of water that whirl and twist over the surface of a lake. They can look like the neck of a monster, weaving to and fro, and this might explain legends of beasts such as the Loch Ness Monster.

DID YOU KNOW?

Hot water freezes more quickly than cold water.

CAN ROCKS FLOAT?

Some rocks float on water. Pumice stone is hardened volcanic lava. It often contains so many air bubbles that it is light enough to float.

WHAT ARE THE NORTHERN LIGHTS?

The aurora borealis, or northern lights, are displays of swirling green and red light high in the night sky near the North Pole. They're caused by charged particles from the solar wind hitting atoms from the Earth's atmosphere, making them emit light.

CAN MUSHROOMS GLOW?

Some fungi glow in the dark and can be seen from 15 m (50 ft) away. They are used as natural lanterns.

IS THE MOON EVER BLUE?

The expression "once in a blue Moon" means that something hardly ever happens. A blue Moon does happen occasionally, though—it happened in 1950 when a large wildfire in Canada sent soot high up into the sky, making the Moon look blue.

DID YOU KNOW?

If you put a drop of oil into a swimming pool, it will spread over the entire surface until it forms a really thin layer.

HOW TOUGH ARE BACTERIA?

Inside the vents of active volcanoes, bacteria live in conditions equivalent to a vat of hydrochloric acid. They're not fussy about their homes!

WHAT IS THE TUNDRA?

The Arctic tundra is a huge, flat, treeless region that has a permanent layer of frost under the ground. The permafrost is 450 m (1,476 ft) deep underground.

WHERE IS THE COLDEST PLACE ON EARTH?

The coldest place on earth is Vostok in Antarctica, where the temperature sometimes falls to almost -90 °C (-129 °F). Unsurprisingly, no one lives there!

DID YOU KNOW?

In 2001, a geologist in India found fossilized raindrops! The imprint was found in ancient rocks, proving that it rained on Earth 1.6 million years ago.

HOW OLD ARE CORAL REEFS

Some cold-water coral reefs have been growing since the end of the last ice age— 10,000 years ago.

HOW BIG ARE BACTERIA?

Most bacteria are tiny—there can be 50 million bacteria in a single drop of liquid. Yet the largest bacterium can just about be seen with the naked eye.

CAN YOU EAT MAMMOTHS?

When polar ice melts, it sometimes reveals mammoths frozen since the end of the last ice age. The mammoth meat can still be fresh—on one occasion, dogs ate the defrosted mammoth before scientists could investigate it!

ARE THERE ANY DINOSAURS WE DON'T KNOW ABOUT?

Scientists believe that 70 percent of dinosaurs are yet to be discovered, since more new species have been found in the last 20 years than ever before.

DID YOU KNOW?

The shell of a lobster is made of chitin—the same substance that mushrooms are made of.

WHERE DID ALL THE ANCIENT ANIMALS GO?

Over 99 percent of all the species in the world that have ever lived are already extinct!

HOW FAR COULD YOU DRAW WITH A PENCIL?

There is enough lead in a pencil to draw a line that is 56 km (35 mi) long. You'd need a good pencil sharpener, though!

WHY DOES KETCHUP GET STUCK IN A BOTTLE?

There's a reason why ketchup won't come out of the bottle and then falls out in a huge dollop—it's called shear thinning. Some thick liquids go thin when shaken, but no one knows exactly how it works and scientists can't predict when it will happen.

HOW FAST IS A COUCH?

Marek Turowski from the UK reached a speed of 148 km/h (92 mph) driving a motorized couch in May 2007.

159

COULD YOU BOUNCE LIGHT OFF THE MOON?

A laser is a very narrow beam of powerful light. It is so straight that it doesn't spread out evenly over huge distances. A laser beam could be reflected off a mirror on the Moon and return back to Earth in a straight line.

IS THERE SUCH A THING AS AN INVISIBILITY CLOAK?

Scientists are working on a "cloak of invisibility" that will hide objects by making light waves flow around them, like water flowing around a rock in a river.

DID YOU KNOW?

Rubber bands last longer if they are kept in a refrigerator.

WHAT IS THE DEEPEST HOLE EVER DUG?

The deepest hole ever dug by humans is in the Kola Peninsula in Russia—the drilling was completed in 1989. It was 12.3 km (7.6 mi) deep.

WHAT IS EARTHRACE?

Earthrace is said to be the world's fastest eco boat. It's partly powered by human fat from its crew members!

HAS THERE EVER BEEN A ROBOT ZOO?

Robotarium X in Portugal was the first zoo full of robots, where 45 robots shared a steel and glass cage. Some were nice and responded to visitors. Others were nasty and bit the tails of their companions. How bizarre!

DID YOU KNOW?

It's impossible to fold a dry piece of paper in half more than seven times. Give it a try!

WHAT METAL WOULD MELT IN YOUR HAND?

The metal gallium melts at body heat— if you held a piece in your hand, it would gradually melt into a pool of liquid.

IS STRIPED TOOTHPASTE BETTER FOR YOUR TEETH?

There is no benefit in using striped toothpaste—the stripes just make the toothpaste look more interesting.

CAN CATS MAKE ELECTRICITY?

If you were to stroke a cat 70 million times, you would generate enough static electricity to power a 60-watt light bulb for one minute. Don't try this one at home ...the poor cat would have no hair left!

DID YOU KNOW?

Recycling one plastic bottle saves enough energy to power a 60-watt light bulb for six hours.

HOW DO YOU MAKE A POISON ARROW?

Some tribes in the Amazon rain forest heat poison arrow frogs over a fire to sweat the poison out of them. They then use the poison to tip their hunting arrows.

DID YOU KNOW?

The National Institute for Standards and Technology in the USA has made an atomic clock as small as a grain of rice.

CAN VULTURES SMELL GAS?

When a gas pipeline leaks in the California desert, workers put a chemical into the gas that attracts turkey vultures. The vultures gather where the gas leaks out, so workers only need to spot the turkey vultures to find the leak.

CAN BLUE LIGHTS KEEP YOU AWAKE?

Scientists are testing the use of blue lights to help keep night drivers awake. They work by convincing the human body clock that it's morning!

DO SMARTPHONES FRIGHTEN GHOSTS?

Reports of ghosts have dropped considerably as the use of smartphones has increased. It seems that the ghouls don't like the radio waves!

WHO INVENTED THE MICROWAVE OVEN?

Percy Spencer (USA) invented the microwave oven in 1945, using new technology developed for military defense during World War II.

DID YOU KNOW?

If a glass of water were magnified to the size of the whole Earth, each molecule would be the size of a tennis ball.

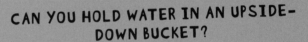

CAN YOU HOLD WATER IN AN UPSIDE-DOWN BUCKET?

If you whirl a bucket of water around fast enough, the water will not fall out, even when the bucket is upside down! This happens because the centrifugal force (which pushes objects outward) is greater than the force of gravity, which would normally cause the water to fall.

CAN WATER CLIMB?

If an electric current is applied to two glasses of water standing next to each other, with the positive electrode in one glass and the negative in the other, the water will climb up the walls of the glass and form a bridge between the two glasses in midair to allow the current to flow.

HOW WERE CATFISH USED BY DOCTORS?

Doctors in ancient Egypt would give patients an electric shock with a catfish to treat the pain caused by arthritis.

WHY DOES COOKING GAS SMELL?

The gas used for cookers and fires has no smell. The gas supply company adds the strong smell deliberately so people can tell immediately if there is a leak.

DO WE BRUSH OUR TEETH WITH SKELETONS?

Many types of toothpaste contain the skeletons of microscopic creatures from the sea, called diatoms.

DID YOU KNOW?

Antifreeze is deadly poisonous—some governments insist that manufacturers add a chemical to make it taste horrible to stop people and animals from drinking it.

IS PITCH SOLID OR LIQUID?

An Australian scientist started a long experiment in 1927 to prove that pitch (a sticky black substance used for waterproofing boats and roofs) is not solid, but a very thick liquid. He put some pitch in a glass funnel and left it to drip through—by 1995, only seven drops had fallen through the funnel!

WHO INVENTED CONCRETE?

Roman engineers were ahead of their time. They heated chalk and seashells at over 900 °C (1,650 °F) to make lime, to which they added volcanic ash, to make concrete.

DID YOU KNOW?

Many people believe that human bodies decay slower than they used to as food is now packed with preservatives that make their way into the flesh—and preserve us, too!

HOW ARE THE HOLES IN CHEESE MADE?

Bubbles of gas produced by bacteria form the holes in Swiss cheese.

CAN PEOPLE EAT ROCKS?

Rock salt is the only rock that humans can eat. It needs to be purified and then ground down into a fine powder before it is added to food.

DO SLUGS WORK LIKE BATTERIES?

The slime produced by a slug produces a small electric current when smeared over copper. Slug-powered phone, anyone?

DID YOU KNOW?

Diamonds are made from the same chemical as the lead in pencils, but the atoms are arranged differently.

WHERE WILL PIGEONS REFUSE TO LAND?

Pigeons won't land on a statue that contains the metal gallium. A Japanese scientist is developing a spray containing gallium that can be used to treat buildings to keep them free from bird droppings.

WHERE DOES THE BEACH BARK?

A beach in Hawaii is named Barking Sands because the sand seems to "bark" like a dog when it's walked on. The dry grains make a strange sound when rubbed together.

WHAT DOES A SMART TOOTHBRUSH DO?

A smart toothbrush uses wireless technology to send information to a screen that can be stuck on a bathroom mirror. The toothbrush monitors and reports back on how well you are brushing and if you've missed any areas!

DID YOU KNOW?

The world's highest limousine was built in Australia and measures 3.33 m (10 ft 11 in) from floor to roof. It took 4,000 hours to build.

CAN BUBBLES FREEZE?

At temperatures below about -25 °C (-13 °F), soap bubbles can freeze in the air and shatter when hitting the ground.

DOES KRYPTONITE EXIST?

Scientists have discovered kryptonite (the fictional mineral supposed to deprive Superman of his powers) in a mine in Serbia. The mineral, known as sodium lithium boron silicate hydroxide, exactly matches the formula of kryptonite in the movie *Superman Returns*.

HOW BIG WERE THE FIRST COMPUTERS?

The first computers used to be so big that they would take up a whole room! By the 1960s, the electronic parts were getting smaller, so they gradually shrank in size. Today, computers can be so tiny that they can fit in the palm of your hand!

DID YOU KNOW?

Recycling one glass bottle saves enough energy to power a computer for 25 minutes.

CAN OXYGEN FREEZE?

Yes, it can! Oxygen turns to a blue liquid at -183 °C (-297 °F). It freezes to a solid at -218 °C (-362 °F).

WHAT WAS THE GRIMMEST JOB IN THE WORLD?

French scientist Antoine-Francois Fourcroy had the lovely job of studying the effects of heat, air, water, and other chemicals on rotting corpses.

169

HOW WAS PEE USED TO LIGHT MATCHES?

Phosphorous (the chemical used for making matches) was first created when chemists extracted it from their urine. The urine was left to stand until it putrefied (went bad). It was later extracted from burned and crushed bones.

CAN YOU MAKE A MAGNET?

Any magnetic material that is touching a magnet starts to behave like a magnet, too! If you attach a paper clip to a magnet, you'll discover that you can attach another one to the first paper clip ... then another ... as many as you like! If you then break the first clip's contact with the real magnet, they will all fall off and lose their "stolen" magnetism!

IS DRINKING WATER SECOND-HAND?

Drinking water has been through many other people's bodies before it gets to you. But don't worry—it's been cleaned!

HOW DO YOU MAKE FERTILIZER?

A traditional old recipe for plant fertilizer consisted of rotten cow dung, ground-up bones, and dry blood. In fact, you can still buy any or all of these or make your own. Or you could just buy a bottle of fertilizer ...

DID YOU KNOW?

Tall buildings are built not to wobble in the wind—but this isn't for safety, it's purely for comfort. People feel unsafe if they can see water sloshing around in the toilet!

WHAT IS A NANOSWIMMER?

Scientists are trying to make nanoswimmers— tiny devices that can swim through blood vessels to keep people healthy or cure illness.

WHAT MAKES BLUE CHEESE SMELLY?

The fungus that gives Stilton cheese its special smell and taste is related to penicillin, an antibiotic that you may take when you're sick.

CAN CARS PLAY TUNES?

Roads in Japan are being built with grooves cut in them, so that if cars drive over them at the right speed, they play a tune!

DID THE BRITISH DESTROY THEIR BEST COMPUTERS?

The first programmable computer, Colossus, was built in England during World War II to crack coded enemy messages. All 14 Colossus computers were destroyed after the war, and the British government denied that they had ever existed.

CAN AIR GUITARS MAKE SOUNDS?

An electronic air guitar device can pick up the movements of your pretend guitar playing and translate them into real guitar sounds.

DID YOU KNOW?

The pyramids in Egypt have moved about 4 km (2.5 mi) to the south since they were built around 5,000 years ago, because the sand they were built on has shifted.

ARE THERE REALLY MAGNET-POWERED TRAINS?

Yes! Maglev trains are able to run at a speed of up to 400 km/h (248 mph). The trains aren't attached to the rails ... they're just pulled along by magnetic force.

WHO IS THE WORLD'S WEIRDEST ARTIST?

German doctor Gunther von Hagens preserves dead bodies and organs for art. He uses a process called plastination to replace body fluids with plastic. The bodies are shown in art exhibitions and are used as learning aids for trainee doctors.

HOW HOT IS THE SUN?

The temperature of the Sun is 6,000 °C (10,832 °F) on the surface and a scorching 15,000,000 °C (27,000,000 °F) in the middle.

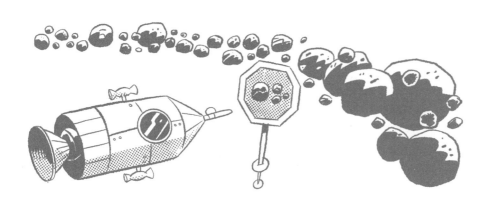

WHAT ARE ASTEROIDS?

Asteroids are small, rocky astronomical objects that orbit the Sun. Hundreds of thousands have been discovered, and they can sometimes behave like planets.

DO ASTRONAUTS WEAR DIAPERS?

Astronauts wear diapers during takeoff, landing, and on space walks, since they can't go to the lavatory at these times!

WHAT HAPPENS WHEN YOU SWEAT IN SPACE?

NASA—the National Aeronautics and Space Administration, founded in the USA in 1958—has developed ways to collect sweat from exercising astronauts to convert into drinking water for them in space. They can also do this with urine!

WHICH IS THE BRIGHTEST PLANET?

Venus is the brightest planet in the Solar System. Yellow clouds made of sulfur and sulfuric acid cover the planet, causing light to reflect off the surface. It is also the hottest planet in the Solar System.

DID YOU KNOW?

Astronauts have to spend time in quarantine before and after they go into space.

WHICH IS THE BEST PLANET FOR BIRTHDAYS?

The best planet to live on if you want a lot of birthdays is Mercury. A year lasts only 88 days, so when you're 10 on Earth you'd be 41-and-a-half on Mercury! But don't worry—instead of living to around 80 years old, you'd live to be 332!

HOW FAST IS THE SOLAR SYSTEM MOVING?

The Solar System travels at 273 km/s (170 mps) around our galaxy, the Milky Way.

HOW DO ASTRONAUTS WASH THEIR HAIR?

Astronauts use special shampoo that they don't have to wash out of their hair.

WHERE DO ASTRONAUTS TRAIN?

NASA uses part of the Arizona desert in the USA to train astronauts. The heat and dust storms make it unpleasant, but the harsh environment is ideal for trying out new equipment and techniques.

WHAT HAPPENS TO POOP IN SPACE?

On the International Space Station, all waste from the lavatories is stored in a supply craft named The Progress. The craft is eventually released and burns away in Earth's atmosphere. Solid waste from space lavatories on shuttles is compressed and stored for return to Earth; liquid waste is thrown out into space.

DID YOU KNOW?

The International Space Station can be seen orbiting the Earth with the naked eye! The best time to look for it is after sunset.